CELEBRATE WITH BOOKS

Literature-Based Whole Language Units For Seasons & Holidays

by Imogene Forte
and
Joy MacKenzie

Incentive Publications, Inc.
Nashville, Tennessee

Illustrations by Gayle Seaberg Harvey
Cover by Becky Ruegger

ISBN 0-86530-190-5

TABLE OF CONTENTS

PREFACE

CELEBRATE WITH BOOKS comprises eleven literature-based, integrated teaching units designed to help teachers help students develop a love for good books, become better readers, acquire skills and concepts in core curriculum areas, and enjoy and appreciate holidays and special days to the fullest.

From "Back to School" with *Miss Nelson is Missing* to anticipation of summer vacation fun with *The Relatives Came*, the thematic units provide cause for celebration of both books and learning-by-doing all year long.

The wide range of activities includes teacher-directed and independent lessons and projects, employing large and small groups, cooperative learning, and individual assignments. All are designed to be easily planned and implemented with a minimum of outside preparation or extensive follow-up.

Book selections are restricted to well-known and easily obtainable books, and materials needed to complete the activities are those ordinarily available in most classrooms.

Each unit includes the following components:

• A creative graphic cover sheet featuring the holiday theme. Teachers can use the cover sheet as a poster, bulletin board display, mobile, booklet cover, or puzzle, or it can be used in other ways to meet individual classroom interests.

• A quick-and-easy teacher's reference section composed of information about:

  • the author
  • the illustrator
  • the story
  • vocabulary
  • the holiday
  • ways to share the book

• A high-interest motivational activity to introduce the unit.

• Curriculum integration activities and projects in related areas including math, science, social studies, music, art, and a full range of whole language experiences.

• A comprehensive culminating activity to reinforce the theme and "tie up" the total experience in a positive and meaningful sense.

In addition to the ten thematic units suitable for holidays and special days throughout the entire school year, a bonus celebration unit suitable for any time of the year has been included for the "special time" when teachers and students just need a cause to celebrate. It is the authors' hope that this combination of special ways to celebrate special days with books and book-related projects will help make the school year an exciting and memorable experience for all concerned.

Back to School.

A Time for New Beginnings

SCHOOL BUS

28

TEACHER OVERVIEW

Miss Nelson Is Missing was written by Harry Allard and illustrated by James Marshall. It is published by Houghton Mifflin Company, Boston, 1977.

THE AUTHOR

Harry Allard was born in 1928. He's a scholar and a bachelor. *Miss Nelson Is Missing* won him the 1980 Georgia Children's Award from the University of Georgia. He began writing when he was only 14 years old, but he attributes his writing career to the encouragement of his longtime friend and fellow writer, James Marshall (the George and Martha Series), who was his collaborator on this book. For fun, he likes to read in French, and he often reads five or six books at the same time. He wrote the third Miss Nelson book one night when he couldn't sleep during a wild storm.

THE ILLUSTRATOR

James Marshall feels lucky to have been born in the forties rather than the fifties because books, rather than television, became the major force in his life. He authored the popular George and Martha Series about a pair of lovable hippos, and he has illustrated dozens of children's books. He says Viola Swamp is based on his second grade teacher, "a horrible woman who laughed at my early creative efforts." She told him he'd never be an artist, so he quit drawing at age seven and didn't take it up again until his late twenties. James speaks French and Italian. His other loves have included an English bulldog and seven cats!

THE STORY

This is the timeless story of a classroom of unruly, mischievous children who take advantage of their attractive teacher's good nature. Her mysterious disappearance leaves them in the inescapable clutches of a vile substitute whom they manage to endure until Miss Nelson suddenly reappears to find a drastically subdued and refreshingly polite and cooperative group of students. The secret of their teacher's mysterious absence is never discovered...or is it?

WORDS TO KNOW

beginning	terrible	secret
missing	arithmetic	*discouraged
friends	school	*misbehave
rude	police	

*bonus (difficult) words

THE THEME: BACK TO SCHOOL – A Time For New Beginnings

Time for a new school year – a time for new beginnings, for growing up, for discovering new ideas, for making new friends. Time to begin a great, new adventure in thinking, imagining, creating, experiencing, and learning.

By the way, who thought of schools in the first place?

Long before there were schoolhouses and hired school teachers, children were taught by parents and grandparents. Young children were sometimes sent to dame schools, where they spent most of their time memorizing Bible passages and reciting them to the dame as she worked on her sewing or knitting. Sometimes ministers held classes in their churches, and in some towns, the minister and the school teacher were the same person.

The first schoolhouses were very uncomfortable. They were often made of logs and had dirt floors. The windows were covered with greased paper instead of glass. In winter, a smoky fire or stove heated the classroom, but those who sat near it were always too hot, and those who sat farthest from it froze. Children had no individual desks. They sat on benches at long, narrow tables, and there was no support for their backs.

Most lessons were written on a slate with chalk. Many children had no paper. Some wrote on birch bark. Pens or charcoal were used instead of pencils. Children were very careful not to soil or lose their books, for it was almost impossible to get new ones.

So schools have not always been the interesting, comfortable, well-equipped places they are today. In most places in the western world, today's schools are designed to provide a friendly, comfortable environment where young people can grow and learn. A new school year is an opportunity, after the relaxation of summer holiday, to begin again with a fresh, new start the process of learning and growing and being part of an enriching community of encouraging grownups and challenging peers.

MOTIVATIONAL ACTIVITY

Use the cover page as a poster or bulletin board display to provoke interest and discussion about school and the beginning of a new school year. Ask students to share with the class what they think is fun or exciting about beginning a new school year. What is dreadful or scary? Ask what they would like to change about schools. What would they do differently if they were the teacher or principal? Emphasize the new opportunities that come with a fresh start and new friends. Ask them to think of a secret that only students in this class can know. Let it be a secret to keep for the whole year. See if they can do it! If so, they might be promised a special event or reward. (Suggestions: The teacher's middle name ... the headmaster's age ... the fact that, once a week, a candy cache is hidden in the room with just enough pieces for each class member. It's a secret from the rest of the school and will last all year – as long as no one tells!)

SHARING THE BOOK

Read the book in one sitting, sharing the pictures, drawing attention to details such as facial expressions. Read to the bottom of page 28, the line that says, "'That's our little secret,' said the kids." Then ask students to consider some of the following questions:

• How did Miss Nelson feel when the students acted rude?

• How does it feel to be a student in a classroom where other students are unruly if you want to cooperate and learn?

• How would it feel to have a mean, strict teacher who never smiled or let you play or do fun things?

• With which kind of teacher do you think you would learn more? With a Miss Nelson or with a Viola Swamp? Explain your answer.

• List some words that describe people who are like:

    Miss Nelson
    Viola Swamp
    Detective McSmogg

• Imagine some additional reasons for Miss Nelson's disappearance.

• What could Miss Nelson's secret be? (If students know, let them enjoy making up some different endings.)

Now, read the last two pages.

• What's your guess? Do you think Miss Nelson's class will remain polite and cooperative, or will they misbehave again?

MATH – "The Numbers Are Missing!"

Each student will need a copy of "The Numbers Are Missing!" work sheet. Each of five story problems is missing a factor or an answer. The missing numbers should be identified and circled in the hidden picture!

THE NUMBERS ARE MISSING!

Name_____ Date_____

Miss Nelson's class has 12 boys and _____ girls.
How many students is that all together? __25__

Every student has a math book except Jody, Peter, and John.
Their books are lost.
How many math books are not lost? _____

Detective McSmogg looked for Miss Nelson in a store, church, bus station, hospital, house, and in four more places.
In how many places did the detective look? _____

Viola Swamp has a very unpleasant last name.
If she changed it to Viola Bluewater, how many more letters would she have to write? _____

Ten of Miss Nelson's students were rude or unkind.
_____ of them apologized.
How many did not apologize? __3__

© 1991 by Incentive Publications, Inc., Nashville, TN.   15

ART & LITERATURE – "Oh! The Thinks You Can Think!"

School is a thinking place! Read aloud to the students Dr. Seuss's *Oh! The Thinks You Can Think!*, place it in a reading center, or arrange to have students take turns reading it aloud in small groups. When the book has been read, provide each student with a copy of the "Oh! The Thinks You Can Think!" work sheet so he or she can illustrate the "most imaginative think he or she can think!"

SCIENCE – "Invisible Names"

Using milk or lemon juice, write the given name of each student on a half sheet of white paper. Pass the papers out to the students at random. Let each assist the teacher in pressing his or her paper with a hot iron until the hidden name appears. The student then takes the paper to the classmate whose name appears. (Younger students may identify the names by matching them with names that label the desks!)
Bonus: When all names have been discovered, ask students to line up across the room in ABC order!

P.S.: Don't forget to discuss the mystery of how the names were written and discovered!

LANGUAGE EXTENSION – "Snapshot"

Distribute to each student the "Snapshot" work sheet showing "photographs" of Miss Nelson's students. Ask them to draw a line to match each picture with the word that fits it best.

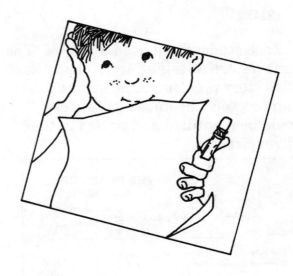

CULMINATING ACTIVITY – "A Time For New Beginnings"

Distribute to each student one copy of the "All About School" work sheet. Ask students to consider each open-ended sentence and complete it thoughtfully. Explain that sharing their answers will give them an opportunity to discuss with the teacher and the class their ideas, their dreams, and suggestions about the school year. (Note: First graders may complete the questionnaire orally.)

ART & WRITING – "Cartoon Couplets"

Provide a copy of "Cartoon Couplets" for each student. Ask students to observe each cartoon and then complete each matching couplet with a rhyming word. Encourage students to create additional cartoons and couplets of their own.

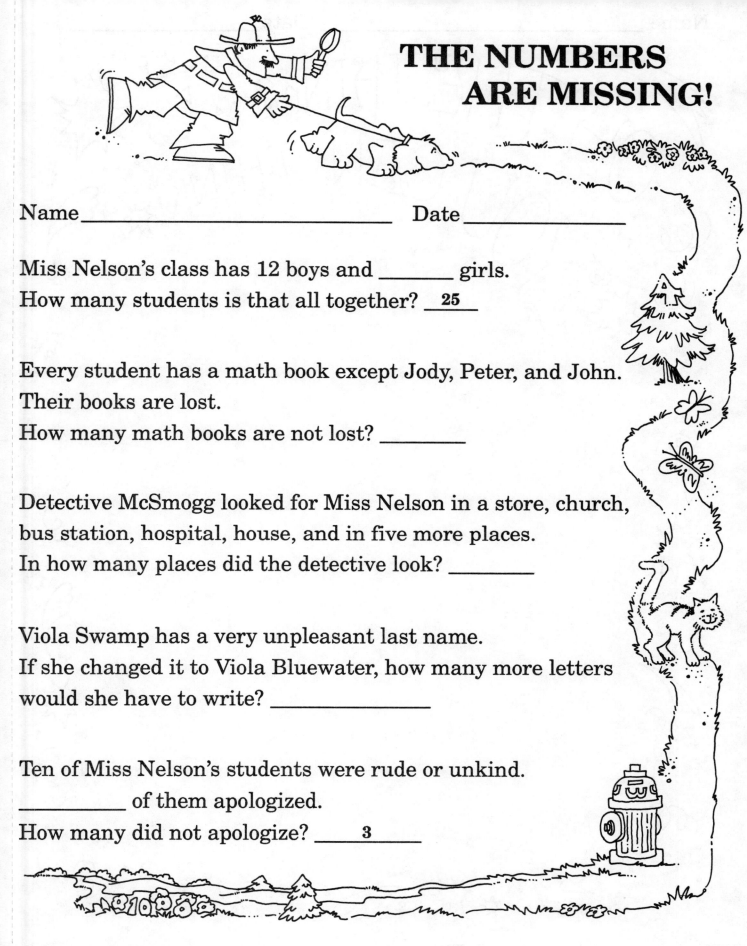

THE NUMBERS ARE MISSING!

Name_____ Date_____

Miss Nelson's class has 12 boys and _____ girls.
How many students is that all together? __25__

Every student has a math book except Jody, Peter, and John.
Their books are lost.
How many math books are not lost? _____

Detective McSmogg looked for Miss Nelson in a store, church,
bus station, hospital, house, and in five more places.
In how many places did the detective look? _____

Viola Swamp has a very unpleasant last name.
If she changed it to Viola Bluewater, how many more letters
would she have to write? _____

Ten of Miss Nelson's students were rude or unkind.
_____ of them apologized.
How many did not apologize? ____3____

OH! THE THINKS YOU CAN THINK!

SNAPSHOT

Name _____ Date_____

Look at the "photographs" of Miss Nelson's students. Draw a line to match each picture with the word that fits it best.

freckled   goofy   giggly   angry
shy   upside down   proud   scared
prissy   sleepy

CARTOON COUPLETS

Name_____ Date_____

If you wanted, I just bet
You could be the teacher's _____!

My teacher is smart, my teacher is wise.
My teacher's head has two sets of _____!

I am shiny, red, and cute!
I'm a teacher's favorite _____!

Our teacher laughed, our teacher roared
When she saw her picture on the _____!

My wonderful teacher deserves a raise.
He's taught me well – I got all _____!

Use the space below to make up a couplet of your own and draw a
cartoon picture to match!

ALL ABOUT SCHOOL

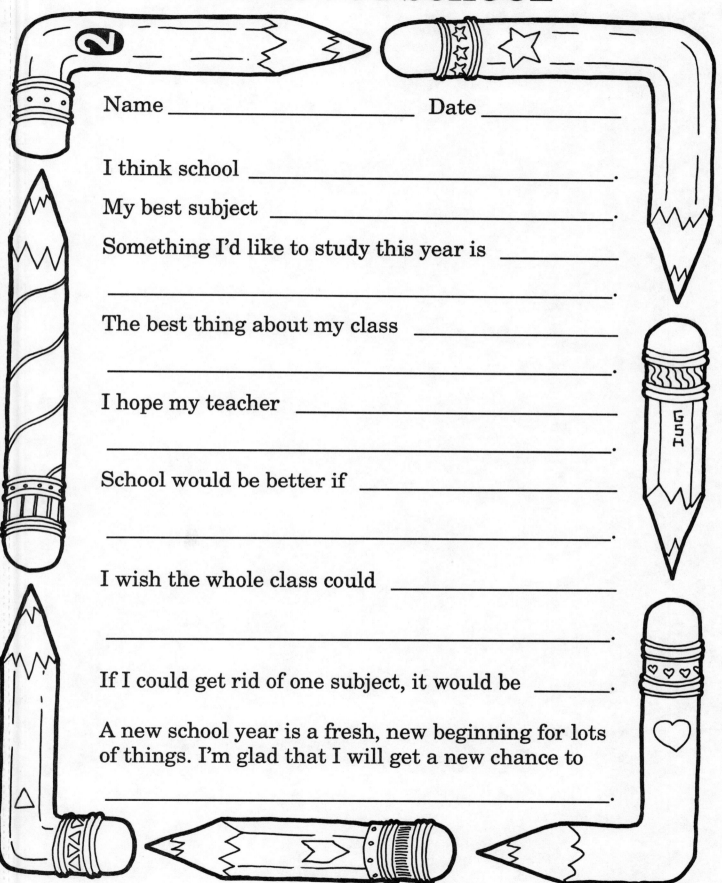

Name _____ Date _____

I think school _____.

My best subject _____.

Something I'd like to study this year is _____

_____.

The best thing about my class _____

_____.

I hope my teacher _____

_____.

School would be better if _____

_____.

I wish the whole class could _____

_____.

If I could get rid of one subject, it would be _____.

A new school year is a fresh, new beginning for lots
of things. I'm glad that I will get a new chance to

_____.

HALLOWEEN
A Time for Tricks and Treats, Enchantment, and Make-Believe

TEACHER OVERVIEW

Heckedy Peg, written by Audrey Wood and illustrated by Don Wood.
Published by Harcourt Brace and Jovanovich, New York, 1987.

THE AUTHOR

Audrey Wood came from a long line of talented family members. She is a fourth generation artist who has illustrated as well as written many children's books. She has owned and operated her own book and import store, taught children's art, and traveled extensively.

THE ILLUSTRATOR

Don Wood is a graduate of the University of California at Santa Barbara and the California College of Arts and Crafts. His work has appeared in many magazines, books, and museum collections.

SOMETHING SPECIAL ABOUT THE WOODS TOGETHER

Audrey and Don Wood are married to each other and presently live with their son Bruce Robert Wood in Santa Barbara, California. Their combined works have enriched the lives of children and adults and have been rewarded by numerous literary awards and honors. They have won the Golden Kite award for illustrations from the Society of Children's Book Writers, the Caldecott Honor Book award, and the New York Times Best Illustrated Children's Book award. Other books by the Woods include the *The Napping House* and *King Bidgood's In The Bath Tub*.

THE STORY

A contemporary story inspired by a sixteenth century game still played by children today, *Heckedy Peg* is a charming, one-of-a-kind story sure to be remembered by young readers and/or listeners. The wicked witch who is missing a leg, and the loving mother whose seven children are named Monday, Tuesday, Wednesday, Thursday, Friday, Saturday, and Sunday are strongly characterized in both words and pictures to highlight the magic and make-believe of the story's rapidly paced plot. Unlike the old woman who lived in a shoe and had so many children she didn't know what to do, this mother knows exactly what to do to make her children happy and to rescue them from the trouble they cause by not obeying instructions during her absence. Without the fanciful word usage and "happy faces" portrayed in the illustrations, parts of the story could be a bit scary for young readers. The multitalented Woods, however, have managed to overshadow the witch's evil intentions with the family's love of life and each other in a merry manner that leaves the reader with a warm feeling and a sense of joy.

WORDS TO KNOW

dusty	stranger	rapped	instead	*overjoyed
market	locked	shouted	chased	*through
careful	suddenly	themselves	onto	*hearth
remember	hobbled	knock	jumped	

*bonus (difficult) words

EXPLORING THE HOLIDAY

THE THEME: HALLOWEEN –
Tricks and Treats,
Enchantment, and
Make-Believe

Of all the holidays, Halloween is looked forward to and considered by many boys and girls as the "most fun holiday of all." The fears and terrors associated with Halloween, as practiced by the cults many, many years ago, have been replaced by colorful costumes, fun parties, and harmless tricks and treats. The customs associated with Halloween in times past grew out of the peoples' fear of darkness. As the days grew shorter, they were afraid that the absence of the sun they worshipped would leave them defenseless against evil powers. To avoid this they burned crops and even some of their animals in bonfires to ward off unkind spirits. As with many other customs and traditions stemming from ignorance and fear, these practices have long since been abandoned and have become a matter of history. Although black cats and witches as Halloween symbols do date back to the time of the cults, their use in Halloween traditions today is for fun and a bit of make-believe magic, not for terror and destruction. Pumpkins, bats, trick-or-treat bags, costumes, and funny faces have been substituted for the grim and grizzly associations of the past.

Whether going door-to-door calling "trick-or-treat" to receive goodie bags filled with wrapped candies and tiny treats, bobbing for apples, or marching in costume parades, children of all ages today look forward to and celebrate Halloween as a time of "tricks and treats, enchantment, and make-believe."

MOTIVATIONAL ACTIVITY

Use the unit cover page as a poster or bulletin board theme to create excitement and motivation for exploring Halloween as a time of tricks and treats, enchantment, and make-believe. Discuss the history and folklore associated with Halloween, and provide time for students to share family and neighborhood customs as well as personal experiences.

SHARING THE BOOK

Before beginning to read the story aloud, capture the children's interest by sharing pictures of the mother, children, and witch, highlighted with a brief description of the setting and characters and a synopsis of the story's major events. Refrain from giving too many clues about the story's ending.

After brief discussion, read the story aloud in one sitting.

POINTS TO PONDER

1. Midway through the story, would you have predicted the end of the story as the author tells it? If not, tell how you thought it was going to end.

2. Since the children were considered to be "such good children" by the mother, why do you think they so readily disobeyed her instructions for the sake of a sack of gold?

3. Which three of the following words would you use to describe the mother? (Choose only three, and explain your choices.)

unselfish	loyal	brave
kind	trusting	thoughtful
caring	ambitious	
responsible	understanding	

CURRICULUM INTEGRATION

MATH – "Seven-Up"

Using the mother's seven children as inspiration for a study of sevens will lead to math fun with a learning bonus. Reproduce, distribute, and provide time for completing the "Seven-Up" work sheet. As a follow-up activity, have students make up "Seven-Up" problems of their own for classmates to solve.

Note: If the problems on the work sheet are not challenging to the ability levels of your students, simply add additional numerals to the 7s to make more difficult problems.

SOCIAL STUDIES – "Family Feelings"

Show pictures of the mother and children and discuss "feelings" shown by their faces. Then reread the story to search for word clues that tell about the family. List words and phrases on the board or a chart, for example, poor mother, good children, overjoyed. Lead a class discussion of the mother's instructions to the children, their disobedience and its causes and consequences, the mother's search for the children and her bravery in attempting their rescue, the children's joy at being reunited as a family, and their love for each other as expressed in the story's happy ending. Extend the discussion to include exploration of family dynamics and their influence, individual commitments of family members to each other, and the responsibilities and benefits of family membership. Conclude the discussion by presenting the "Family Feelings" work sheet. Ask students to think of the qualities that make their own families special and to complete the work sheet accordingly.

SCIENCE – "Blowing Bubbles"

Provide large bowls of water, liquid dishwashing detergent, and a collection of small objects to be used for blowing bubbles (spools, slotted spoons, combs, small paper tubes, etc.). Cover work surfaces with newspaper to avoid water damage and encourage students to experiment with blowing bubbles. Observe and discuss how the bubbles are formed, colors, what happens when the bubbles "dissolve," and other wonders of the bubble-blowing process. Ask students to look at the bubble-blowing scene illustrated in the book and discuss why the children waited until the mother was away to blow bubbles.

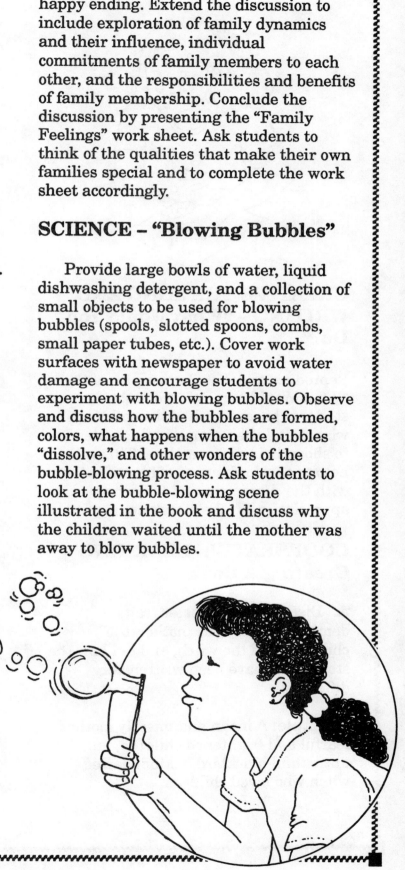

CREATIVE THINKING AND WRITING – "What Would You Do?"

Reproduce and distribute copies of the "What Would You Do?" work sheet. Ask students to read each of the children's wishes and then complete the sentences to show their own reactions. This will help to develop a sense of identification with the characters and to deepen appreciation for the story's ending.

COOPERATIVE LEARNING – Creating A Book

A. Discuss the character traits demonstrated by the mother, the children, and the witch, and tell how the story could have been written very differently.

Example: A mean and miserly mother, fearful and frightened children, an untruthful blackbird, a kindhearted witch who loved children.

B. Divide students into groups of five. Ask each group to:

1. Review the story as told by the author.

2. Discuss the character traits.

3. Write a new story based on the same plot as that presented in the story but with a different sequence of events and ending based on character changes devised by the group.

4. Write the story as acceptable to your group. Then edit it, copy it, illustrate it, and prepare a cover for it. Add the completed copy to the free-reading table.

CULMINATING ACTIVITY – "Tricks and Treats, Enchantment and Make-Believe"

Discuss each of the characters as portrayed by the author and illustrator, and discuss how each character contributed to the story's feeling of tricks and treats, enchantment, and make-believe.

SEVEN-UP

Name_____ Date _____

$$\begin{array}{r} 7 \\ +7 \\ \hline \end{array} \qquad \begin{array}{r} 7 \\ -7 \\ \hline \end{array} \qquad \begin{array}{r} 7 \\ \times 7 \\ \hline \end{array}$$

$$\begin{array}{r} 17 \\ +7 \\ \hline \end{array} \qquad \begin{array}{r} 17 \\ -7 \\ \hline \end{array} \qquad \begin{array}{r} 17 \\ \times 7 \\ \hline \end{array}$$

$$\begin{array}{r} 77 \\ +17 \\ \hline \end{array} \qquad \begin{array}{r} 77 \\ -17 \\ \hline \end{array} \qquad \begin{array}{r} 77 \\ \times 17 \\ \hline \end{array}$$

$7 + 7 \times 7 - 7 =$

$17 + 17 \times 17 - 17 =$

$77 + 7 \times 7 - 7 =$

Make up 7 Seven-Up problems of your own. Solve them.

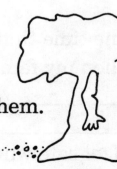

FAMILY FEELINGS

Name_____ Date_____

Here is a picture of my family and me doing some things that make me feel very special.

I made someone in my family feel very proud when _____

_____

_____ .

One time that I will always remember feeling _____ was when my family and I _____

_____

_____ .

I feel safe when I know that my family is _____

_____ .

WHAT WOULD YOU DO?

Name _____ Date _____

Each of the children in *Heckedy Peg* knew exactly
what he or she wanted from the market.
Write about what you would do with each of the things
they asked for.

Monday asked for a tub of butter.
"If I had a tub of butter, I would _____
_____.

Tuesday asked for a pocketknife.
"With a pocketknife of my own, I would _____
_____.

Wednesday asked for a china pitcher.
"If someone gave me a china pitcher, _____
_____.

Thursday asked for a pot of honey.
"I would share a pot of honey _____
_____.

Friday asked for a tin of salt.
"Oh dear! If I had a tin of salt, _____
_____.

Saturday asked for crackers.
"With crackers I would surely want _____
_____.

Sunday asked for a bowl of egg pudding.
"A bowl of egg pudding would be nice, but_____
_____.

TEACHER OVERVIEW

How Many Days To America? A Thanksgiving Story, written by Eve Bunting and illustrated by Beth Peck. Published by Clarion Books, New York, 1988.

THE AUTHOR

Eve Bunting was born and educated in Ireland and now lives in Pasadena, California. She has written over fifty popular picture books for children and young adults. She was the winner of the Golden Hite Award from the Society of Children's Book Writers in 1976 for *One More Flight*, and she has been recognized for the ALA Best Book for Young Artists. Among her notable titles are *The Mother's Day Mice; Scary, Scary Halloween; The Valentine Bears; The Man Who Could Call Down Owls;* and *Ghost's Hour, Spook's Hour.*

THE ILLUSTRATOR

Beth Peck lives in New York City with her husband and two cats. She studied at Rhode Island School of Design and attends classes at the Art Students League and the National Academy of Design.

THE STORY

Told from a child's point of view, this contemporary Thanksgiving story tells of refugees from a Caribbean island embarking on a dangerous boat trip to America, where they have a special reason to celebrate the holiday. It is a heartwarming and courageous story of people willing to risk danger and uncertainty to find safety and freedom. The author uses subtle imagery to create a vivid background for the story without wordy detail. Much is said about caring, hardship, and hope for a better way of life. The artist uses pastels effectively to illustrate pain, determination, and love. *How Many Days To America?* is a reflective book for all ages. It presents the Thanksgiving theme for all races, time, and seasons and offers children an understanding of family love, faith, and courage.

WORDS TO KNOW

soldiers	shore	clasped
wisp	direction	huddled
quay	bow	*village
garnet	silent	*scrambled
harbor	surf	*sighted

*bonus (difficult) words

THE THEME: THANKSGIVING – A Time To Be Thankful

The pilgrims who first celebrated Thanksgiving Day in the Plymouth Colony in 1621 would be surprised indeed to attend a typical Thanksgiving dinner in America today. As they feasted on wild turkeys and quail fresh from the hunt, supplemented by pumpkins, squash, and yellow corn meal mush, they could hardly have dreamed that this simple feast would set the stage for a legal holiday to be observed for centuries to come. The pilgrims came from England to America looking for a better life and for the freedom to live this new life as they saw fit. The first winter was cold and hard, and almost half of the original settlers died. The remaining hardy souls planted the corn they brought with them and discovered other meager food stuffs growing in this new homeland. They built shelters to protect them from the harsh weather and settled in to start new lives of freedom.

Governor William Bradford set aside a time for giving thanks to God for the blessings of food, shelter, and freedom. For three days the grateful pilgrims and their native American guests sang, prayed, and shared the beauty of their new land.

Today, this first Thanksgiving is remembered and honored by families from sea to shining sea as a time for homecoming, for renewing family ties, and for giving thanks. Pumpkin, squash, turkey, and cornbread dressing are served today as then, but cakes, candies, casseroles, jellies, pickles, and many more food specialties have been added to Thanksgiving menus. Almost every family has its own special Thanksgiving dishes and traditions, and like the families themselves, these grow more varied and interesting as the years come and go. One thing remains the same – Thanksgiving is a time to be thankful!

MOTIVATIONAL ACTIVITY

Review the history and traditions associated with Thanksgiving and provide time for students to share things for which they are especially thankful this year. Set aside a space on the free-reading table for books about Thanksgiving. Show and discuss several books, including poetry, song, history, literature, and things-to-make books. Place the books in the designated space, and remind students to enjoy them during free time.

SHARING THE BOOK

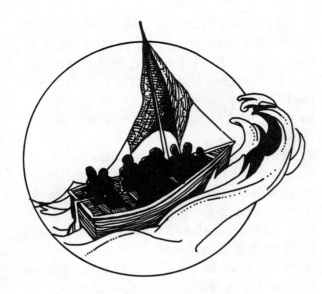

Before reading the book aloud, briefly share the original Thanksgiving story, emphasizing reasons for the journey and hardships faced by the families in search of freedom. Discuss other times in history when people left their homes to find a better place to live. Share book illustrations to introduce the setting and characters of the story. Read the story in one sitting.

POINTS TO PONDER

1. How do you think this book relates to the original Thanksgiving story? Compare likenesses and differences in story events.

2. Does the author tell directly how the people felt during their journey, or does she leave room for imagination? Use lines from the story to illustrate images of fear, love, and courage.

3. When the father said that they must leave because they did not think the way the soldiers thought, what do you think he meant? Why was he afraid for his family? Why did they hurry and move silently along the secret streets?

4. Which of these emotions describes the boy's feelings during the journey?

happiness	longing	kindness
fear	hunger	joy
excitement	confusion	playfulness
sadness	security	

5. The characters in this story were not given names. Why do you think this was done?

6. The sister asked many questions during the trip. What would you have asked?

CURRICULUM INTEGRATION

Freedom

SOCIAL STUDIES – "Searching For Freedom"

As a group, find the definitions of "free," "freedom," and "liberty" in the dictionary. Make a list of rights enjoyed in a free country. Lead a discussion of how we would feel if our country did not allow the rights to think, speak, or worship as we wish. Discuss these freedoms and personalize them as they relate to everyday education, shopping, eating, voting, television, books, dress, and friendships. Reproduce and distribute the "Favorite Freedoms" work sheet. Allow time for students to complete and share their answers. Compare the answers and discuss the freedom to have similar and differing responses.

MATH – "Numbers For Thanksgiving"

Practice computation and math comprehension skills. Encourage the students to work the word problems created for *How Many Days To America?* and the original Pilgrim Thanksgiving story. Reproduce and distribute the "Numbers for Thanksgiving" work sheet.

For an extended activity, lead the students in creating their own math word problems based on Thanksgiving customs and celebrations.

Note: Number facts used for these problems are not based on historical data.

COOPERATIVE LEARNING – "Then And Now"

Provide resource books containing information about the original Thanksgiving story. Divide the class into groups of five.

1. Ask each group to read and discuss one of the Thanksgiving book selections and list two Thanksgiving facts.

2. Allow time for groups to illustrate their information.

3. Compile the lists for a class book about Thanksgiving.

4. Extend the book's coverage by creating a section on "Thanksgiving Today" by asking each group to provide a list representing Thanksgiving celebrations in their own homes.

LANGUAGE – "Examining Images"

Present the following lines from the book and lead a group discussion of imagery. Define and give examples of the term "image."

...I could see my mother's feet in their black slippers and the great muddy boots of the soldiers.

...Others, too, moved silently along the secret streets.

...We chugged heavily from harbor to open ocean.

...Her face twisted the way it did when she closed the door of our home for the last time.

...Day followed night and night, day.
...Fear moved like a bad wind between us.
...There was such a silence among us then, such an anxious, watchful silence.

...Though the benches were crowded, there was room for all of us.
...My father's song lost itself in the wind.

ART – "Time To Dream"

The boy in *How Many Days To America?* dreamed of home, food, and an uncle while he was on the boat coming to America. Provide mural paper and art supplies and allow students to draw things and people they would dream about on such a journey.

CULMINATING ACTIVITY: – "A Time To Be Thankful"

Summarize the story and its application to the celebration of the American Thanksgiving. Use the lines of the song that the father sang to reassure the boy of the purpose of their dangerous journey.

"Sleep and dream, tomorrow comes
And we shall all be free."

Relate the boy's comment of "it is the coming-to-America day" to the celebration of the first Thanksgiving. Lead a discussion of the meaning of freedom and the right to celebrate holidays as we see fit as privileges taken for granted by people living in a free country. Ask students to name things often taken for granted.

FAVORITE FREEDOMS

☆ Freedom ☆ Freedom ☆ Freedom ☆ Freedom ☆ Freedom ☆ ☆

Name ______________________ Date ________________

During my "free" time I have the right to:

Read ____

____.

Watch ____

____.

Say ____

____.

Play ____

____.

Dress in my _____________________________________

____.

Eat ____

____.

Buy ____

____.

Worship ____

____.

Be with ____

____.

Listen to _______________________________________

____.

My favorite freedom of all is the freedom to ____________

____.

NUMBERS FOR THANKSGIVING

Name _____ Date _____

1. The boy in the story had a sister, a mother, and a father. If there were twenty-three other people traveling with them, how many people were going to America? _____

2. If there had been 102 pilgrims on the Mayflower and only half the group survived the first year, how many pilgrims celebrated the second Thanksgiving? _____

3. Each family on the small boat received two papayas, three lemons, and a coconut from the soldiers. There were six families on the boat. How many pieces of fruit were distributed? _____

4. If the pilgrims sailed for eight weeks before sighting America, how many days did they sail? _____

5. The first American Thanksgiving was in 1621. How many years ago was it first celebrated? _____

6. Once on American soil, the boy's family was given plenty to eat. There was enough bread for two slices per person. Use your answer in question **1** to find how many slices of bread were served. _____

TEACHER OVERVIEW

Frederick was written and illustrated by Leo Lionni. It was first published by Pantheon Books, Random House in 1967. The Pinwheel Books paperback edition appeared in March 1973.

THE AUTHOR/ILLUSTRATOR

Leo Lionni is not only a writer but also a designer and painter. He was born in Amsterdam, Holland, but he became a United States citizen in 1939. He holds two Caldecott Medal Runner-up Awards for *Swimmy* and *Frederick*. He says, "I don't make books for children. I make them for that part of us, of myself and my friends, which has never changed, which is still a child." He has two grown children of his own. His greatest regret in life is that he did not learn to play a musical instrument well.

THE STORY

This charming story of a tiny field mouse not only delights the natural taste and curiosity of young readers but also subtly and beautifully reinforces the flow of nature toward artistic expression. It makes poets natural heroes! The mice in the story are all busy "storing up" for winter, but it seems Frederick is not. He sits and dreams in the sun and does his own kind of "storing." When the long, cold winter days arrive, the other mice have corn, nuts, and wheat to share. Only Frederick has warmth and color to chase away the cold and gray. Only Frederick has words and ideas to fill the long winter days with charm and excitement.

WORDS TO KNOW

winter	magic	poet
cold	Frederick	*applauded
snow	nibbled	*abandoned
store	memories	*granary
supplies	hideout	*periwinkles

*bonus (difficult) words

EXPLORING THE HOLIDAY

THE THEME: WINTER – A Time To Rest and Restore

In the natural world, winter is a time of rest and dormancy for many plants and animals, a time of gathering and storing, a time to prepare for the bloom and birth of spring.

In the world of human beings, winter can provide some of the same kinds of advantages and opportunities. It can be a time to rest, relax, restore, and regenerate. It's a great time for thinking, reading, and writing for one's own pleasure.

Suggest that students keep a winter journal. They might like to record natural events such as weather, storms, depth of snow, windspeed on various days, descriptions of the landscape, sketches of winter birds and animals, insects found hiding in hollow logs, snowflakes, or frosted windows. Winter has many mysteries that are fun to explore, things such as hibernating snakes, snow crystals, animals tracks, winter camouflages, flight patterns of birds, and unusual animal activity on beaches.

Then there are always the special ice and snow games, crackling fires, and warm kitchens where spicy smells and tastes abound.

Encourage students to greet the winter season with curiosity and anticipation and to plan several exciting group and individual projects that will make long, gray winter days a time to look forward to.

MOTIVATIONAL ACTIVITY

Use the cover page to create a poster or bulletin board showing some of the excitement and mystery of winter activity. Discuss with students the environmental changes that take place with the arrival of the winter season. Using a world map for reference, point out that winter arrives at different times in different parts of the world. Let students share their favorite things about winter as they work together to make hot chocolate, popcorn, or caramel apples!

SHARING THE BOOK

Assign student readers to read parts of the story using clear enunciation and creative oral expression.

Share the story with the entire class, allowing each reader, in turn, to hold his or her page for the class to see as he or she reads. After the first reading, ask a few of the listeners to identify their favorite part of the story. Then discuss Frederick's unusual "store" of things. A second reading may be done by allowing the first readers to choose replacements for themselves.

POINT TO PONDER
How are people and animals alike in the ways they prepare for winter?

Animals
- Gathering and storing food
- Making nests, underground caves
- Moving south
- Growing warmer coats and coverings
- (Frederick) – gathering words, colors, and feelings to remember

People
- Canning and freezing food
- Gathering firewood, making homes warm and tight with storm windows, etc.
- Going to warmer climates
- Using warmer blankets and clothing

- Gathering memories, good books, and indoor entertainment such as puzzles.

CURRICULUM INTEGRATION

SCIENCE – "Winter Hideouts"

Reproduce and distribute to each student copies of the "Winter Hideouts" work sheets. Read and discuss together as a class the information on the animal page. Then ask students to cut out the animals and place each in its proper winter "hideout" on "Winter Hideouts" page 2.

MATH – "Hey, Mr. Scientist!"

Make a copy of the "Hey, Mr. Scientist!" math riddle sheet. Show younger or less-able students how to "break the code." Allow others to work independently to solve the problems, use the solutions to break the code, and find the answer to the riddle.

ART – "Psychedelic Socks"

Winter is a time to cover frosty toes with warm socks. Here's a fun art project that will tickle the toes as well as the fancy!

This activity may be done using bare feet or a pair of old socks. If socks are used, mismatched ones are fine, and students may be asked to bring a pair from home. Use wide, washable, felt-tip markers to create psychedelic slipper socks by painting wild, sock-and-shoe designs directly on bare feet or on a pair of socks. To allow for mistakes, designs should be done first with a very light color, then retraced in strong, bright colors. Have a "foot show" and take pictures!

LANGUAGE/WRITING – "Poems For Frederick"

One of the most surprising and delightful things about Frederick is that he turns out to be a poet. Reread the next-to-last page of *Frederick* and listen for the rhyme in Frederick's poems. Clap the lines together. Then listen for the rhyme words.

Ask students to compose their own four-line rhymes about winter. Make a bulletin board entitled "Winter Poems for Frederick." Use the row of mice at the bottom of the poetry page as a pattern to decorate your board. Ask students to display finished poetry on the board.

LITERATURE EXTENSION/ART – "Wild And Wonderful Winter Weather"

For most places in the world, winter is a time for all sorts of wild, wonderful, unpredictable weather. Read aloud to the class the book *Cloudy with a Chance of Meatballs* by Judi Barrett (Atheneum). Let the students enjoy the fanciful tale. Then ask them to think first as a class, then individually, of alliterative, tongue-twister phrases that could describe the kinds of weather in the book. (Example: puddle of pasta, peas, and porridge. Meatball madness and mustard mess.) Each student should then choose one favorite tongue twister and use it as a caption for a fanciful weather picture, similar to the ones in the book. Be sure to provide a display area for the finished products.

CULMINATING ACTIVITY – "A Time To Rest And Restore"

On a cold winter day, there is nothing as nice to feel, smell, and taste as a big, warm gingerbread cookie!

Divide students into several working groups. Provide each group with the recipe, tools, and ingredients to make giant gingerbread people. Ask groups to work together to follow directions and create their "gingerbread giants." When the baking is done, allow groups to enjoy their cookies with milk or juice and celebrate winter as a time to rest and restore.

WINTER HIDEOUT

Name _____

Date _____

The bear takes a long, lazy nap in a cave or in a hideout under low-hanging trees. Shh! You might wake him if you're noisy!

Field mice make cozy nests lined with grass. They dig tunnels through the dirt and snow to places where they can find roots and seeds for food.

Beavers store their winter food under the water. Their thick coats keep them warm even under the ice of frozen ponds and streams.

Snakes like to curl up together – sometimes thousands of them – in the same underground nest. Just before bedtime, they eat a big meal that lasts them through their long, winter nap.

A raccoon may make himself a cozy nest of leaves or woodchips in a hollow tree. He sleeps only in very cold weather, so you may meet him on a winter walk.

Moles are happy underground all year-round. They live on roots of grass and trees.

Bats sleep hanging upside down by their feet from the cave ceiling. What a strange way to spend the winter!

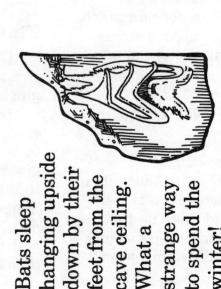

Toads bury themselves in mud and breathe lightly through their skin.

Page 2

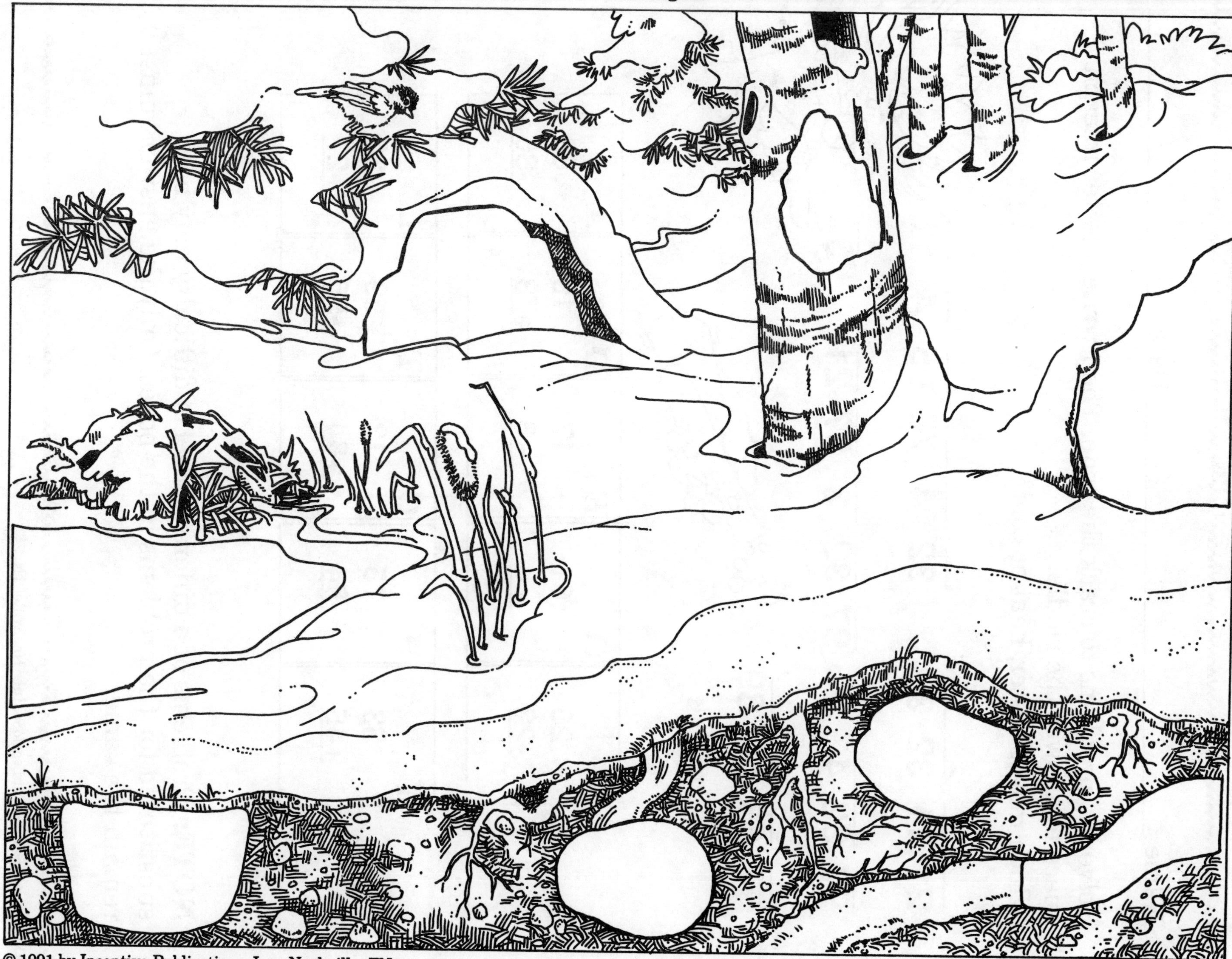

HEY, MR. SCIENTIST!

Name _____ Date _____

Solve the problems to crack the code. Then write a letter in each space to answer the riddle.

Which moves faster, heat or cold?

$\overline{21}$ $\overline{11}$ $\overline{32}$ $\overline{3}$ **!** $\overline{32}$ $\overline{4}$ $\overline{78}$ $\overline{65}$ $\overline{4}$ $\overline{11}$

$\overline{97}$ $\overline{32}$ $\overline{4}$ $\overline{97}$ $\overline{32}$ $\overline{3}$ $\overline{97}$ $\overline{21}$ $\overline{32}$

$\overline{97}$ $\overline{65}$ $\overline{59}$ $\overline{89}$ **.**

N	O	E	D	A
26 -22	61 $+\ 4$	17 $-\ 6$	16 $+73$	68 -36

Y	H	C	T	L
33 $+45$	75 -54	13 $+84$	59 -56	32 $+27$

NOTE: Problems of a different level of difficulty may be substituted for the problems in the boxes. Only the answers must remain the same.

GINGERBREAD GIANTS

Name_____ Date_____

1 box of gingerbread mix   cookie sheet   pot holder
1/3 cup of warm water   mixing bowl   raisins
measuring cup   shortening   paper towel
spoon

Optional: *You may use frosting or candies to make a scarf, hat, or socks and mittens on your giant.*

1. Pour mix into the bowl.
2. Add water and stir until mixture is wet.
3. Put the bowl of dough in the refrigerator for about 20 minutes.
4. Preheat oven to 375°.
5. Use the paper towel and shortening to grease the cookie sheet.
6. Remove dough from the refrigerator.
7. Roll one ball of dough for a head, and press down flat on the cookie sheet.
8. Roll a larger ball for a body, and press it flat on the cookie sheet.
9. Roll two logs for arms and two larger logs for legs. Press the arms and legs in place.
10. Add raisin eyes, mouth, and buttons.
11. Bake for 15-20 minutes or until golden brown.

CHRTSTMAS
·A Time of Excitement and Imagination·

TEACHER OVERVIEW

How the Grinch Stole Christmas, written and illustrated by Dr. Seuss.
Originally published by Random House, New York, 1957.

THE AUTHOR/ILLUSTRATOR

Millions of Dr. Seuss fans, including young children, adolescents, teenagers, adults, and seniors, have enjoyed the fruits of this talented writer's labors for well over a quarter of a century. Not all of his readers know that in real life Theodore Seuss Gisell is in his late eighties and enjoys life immensely from a hilltop home in LaJolla, California. Among other honors, Dr. Seuss has been awarded a Pulitzer Prize Special Citation, doctorates in literature and fine arts from several universities, and virtually every prestigious children's book award, two Emmys, and a Peabody award for his work in film. His *Cat In The Hat* books, featuring high interest/low vocabulary themes, have put fun into beginning reading. Perhaps more than anything else, however, Dr. Seuss will be remembered for the unique characters, imaginative settings and illustrations, and especially the creative word usage that characterizes the magical world of words he continues to create for children of all ages.

THE STORY

An all-time favorite Christmas classic that continues to delight children year after year, this book is in a category all by itself. It represents Dr. Seuss at his best. As the growling Grinch plots and plans a great Grinchy trick to spoil Christmas for all the Whos living in Whoville, the happy Whos prove that Christmas is indeed much more than goodies and gimmicks. With the help of a fake reindeer (also known as dog Max), some bags and old empty sacks, and a ramshackle sleigh, the Grinch sails into Whoville as all the Whos snooze, and what happens next is something a Grinch would "never choose." After all the toys, presents, stockings and treats, and even the Christmas feast are loaded up the chimney, into the sled, and whisked away up to the top of Mt. Crumpit, the Grinch discovers to his amazement that the Whos go right ahead with a Christmas that's as merry as can be. Their singing and celebrating, without any presents at all, leave the Grinch puzzled and pondering. The story's happy ending leaves the Whos, the Grinch, and the reader with a warm feeling for Whos, Grinches, and especially for Christmas Day. It's a read-aloud book not to be missed.

WORDS TO KNOW

reason	growled	heart	surprise
season	noise	awful	shocking
hated	puzzled	dreaming	*nimbly
presents	feast	more	*reindeer
wrath	singing	glee	*ramshackle
stockings	wonderful	merry	

*bonus (difficult) words

EXPLORING THE HOLIDAY

THE THEME: CHRISTMAS – A Time Of Excitement And Imagination

Christmas is perhaps the most widely celebrated holiday of the whole year. People in many different countries celebrate Christmas in many different ways. The traditional focus of the Christmas holiday is to mark the birth of Jesus Christ in a stable in Bethlehem more than 2000 years ago. In the years since that time, groups of people all over the world have established widely varying Christmas customs and traditions. Celebrations range from midnight church services, plum pudding, and banquet tables to parades, pinatas, stockings for Santa to fill, and switches and ashes for bad children. Almost all customs still incorporate a babe in a manger, a kindly figure bearing gifts and treats, decorations and delicacies, and family gatherings. Apart from these common elements, however, national, ethnic, and community groups have devised as many differing ways to celebrate this holiday as there are languages to say "Merry Christmas!" Whether it is with a star shining brightly over a manger, a bevy of jolly little elves and a reindeer with a red nose, a yule log or holly tree, or a "Ho, ho, ho!" and a bag of toys, there is one thing you can count on. Wherever and however Christmas is celebrated the world over, it continues to be a time of excitement and imagination.

MOTIVATIONAL ACTIVITY

Discuss the history and customs associated with the Christmas holiday, and encourage students to share personal insights and experiences.

Reproduce and distribute copies of the unit cover page. Ask students to:

1. Find and color six wrapped packages hiding in the picture.

2. Draw three more packages under the tree.

3. Color the picture.

4. Discuss with the group the gift that might be in each package.

5. Take the picture home to share with family members.

SHARING THE BOOK

Read the book in one sitting at the beginning of the Christmas season.

Then place it on the free-reading table, where its presence will surely add excitement and imagination to the holiday festivities.

Like all Dr. Seuss books, *How The Grinch Stole Christmas* is a book to be enjoyed, savored, and treasured. Long after the figurative language has been pittered and pattered, the giggles have quieted, and the characters portrayed in both dialogue and drama, the story's lively plot and sequence will draw the listener back to the book again and again. The vocabulary itself makes the book both magnetic and manageable for young readers. Key words are repeated throughout the story and are visually reinforced by highly detailed two-color illustrations and context clues.

Draw attention to appropriate pages as the suggested curriculum activities are presented, and ask students to elaborate on and extend the scenes and scenarios as presented.

Students might be asked to:

A. Select roles to "act out."

B. Make a list of words to describe the Grinch, Max, Little Cindy Lou Who, the ramshackle sleigh, the Grinch's cave, and the roast beast.

C. Sing a few favorite Christmas songs in honor of the Whos' Christmas sing.

POINTS TO PONDER

1. What could have happened to the Grinch to make him feel so mean about Christmas?

2. Why do you think the Grinch hated the whole season, not just Christmas Day?

3. What kind of town was Whoville? Was it a tiny village, a seaside or mountain community, a small town, or a big city?

4. How must Max have felt about having a horn tied to the top of his head and being hitched to a sled?

5. Do you think Whoville would have been a good place to live? Why?

6. What kind of toys would the children of Whoville have asked Santa for?

7. What changes (if any), would the Grinch have made in his attitude and behavior toward other people after he shared Christmas with the Whos?

SCIENCE – "Weather Watch"

Ask students to search the book for clues related to the weather in Whoville on Christmas Eve when the Grinch came down from his cave to steal Christmas. Discuss the temperature necessary for snow, what causes snow to fall, what snowflakes look and feel like, and how long snow usually has to fall before the rooftops and ground are covered. Provide a world map and help students locate parts of the world that have heavy snows for long periods of time and parts of the world that have little or no snow. Discuss weather in your own location and evaluate the possibility of a "white Christmas."

SOCIAL STUDIES – "A Grinch's Celebration"

Reproduce and distribute copies of the "A Grinch's Celebration" work sheet. Discuss the part of the story related to the Grinch's appreciation of Christmas after the Whos introduced him to the true meaning of the holiday. Provide time for completion of the work sheet.

BULLETIN BOARD DISPLAY – "A Grinch's Celebration In Living Color"

Provide large sheets of drawing paper and crayons or markers. Ask students to illustrate the celebration they have just planned on the work sheet. Display the completed work sheets and illustrations on a bulletin board. (See bulletin board sketch on page 58.)

ART – "Suited To Size"

Distribute copies of the "Suited To Size" work sheet and ask students to challenge their imaginations to design a Santa suit for the Grinch.

MATH – "Who-Pudding, Who-Hash, And Who Knows What Else"

To reinforce the use of measurement terms and their meaning, ask students to make up original recipes for food items the Whos might have prepared for the Christmas feast. Provide a supply of cookbooks and magazines with colorfully illustrated holiday recipes to be used for reference and inspiration. Compile the completed holiday recipes into a recipe book. If possible, prepare and enjoy a "Who Feast" as part of the celebration.

LITERATURE BONUS

Place a copy of *A Snowy Day* on the free-reading table. This beautifully illustrated book will provide a visual feast for young readers.

WRITING – "What, Why, And How"

Reproduce and distribute copies of the "What, Why, and How" work sheet. Ask students to follow directions for creative self-expression.

LANGUAGE BONUS/WORD APPRECIATION – "Who Words"

Discuss Dr. Seuss's creative use of language in this and some of his other books. Make available a good collection of Dr. Seuss books for free reading if possible. Ask students to repeat with you some of the more figurative language usage, and have fun making up other ways to use the words and phrases.

Distribute the "Who Words" work sheet and ask students to share completed sentences.

CREATIVE THINKING – "What If..."

Distribute the "What If ..." work sheet and provide time for students to brainstorm and complete the work sheet as a "partners project." Display the completed "picture stories" on the bulletin board.

CULMINATING ACTIVITY – "A Time Of Excitement And Imagination"

Provide rhythm band instruments and ask students to improvise sounds they think the Whos of Whoville might have made to add to the noise that the Grinch hated most of all. After each student has had time to experiment and devise his or her own sound, ask students to blend the sounds into a "Noise! Noise! Noise!" march, and stage a gala parade.

As a good finale to the parade, enjoy an old-fashioned "sing-along." Distribute copies of the "We Wish You A Merry Christmas" work sheet. Enjoy the song at the end of the "sing-along." Then provide time for students to complete the work sheet and color it. This will make another great "take-home" and a festive wrap-up for the "Christmas, A Time Of Excitement And Imagination" unit.

A GRINCH'S CELEBRATION

Name_____ Date _____

Just suppose the Grinch learned to love Christmas as much as the Whos in Whoville. With no past experience, he would need help in planning the celebration.

Complete the lists below to help out.

GRINCH'S GIFT LIST

MAYOR OF WHOVILLE: _____

CINDY-LOU WHO: _____

A JUST-MADE FRIEND: _____

DOG MAX: _____

GRANNY GRINCH: _____

A WHO, WHOSE CUPBOARD IS BARE: _____

NEIGHBOR, NORTH OF WHO-VILLE: _____

THE CAROLERS: _____

ENTERTAINMENT

STORY

GAMES

Christmas Dinner Menu

A GRINCH'S CELEBRATION IN LIVING COLOR

Bulletin Board Display

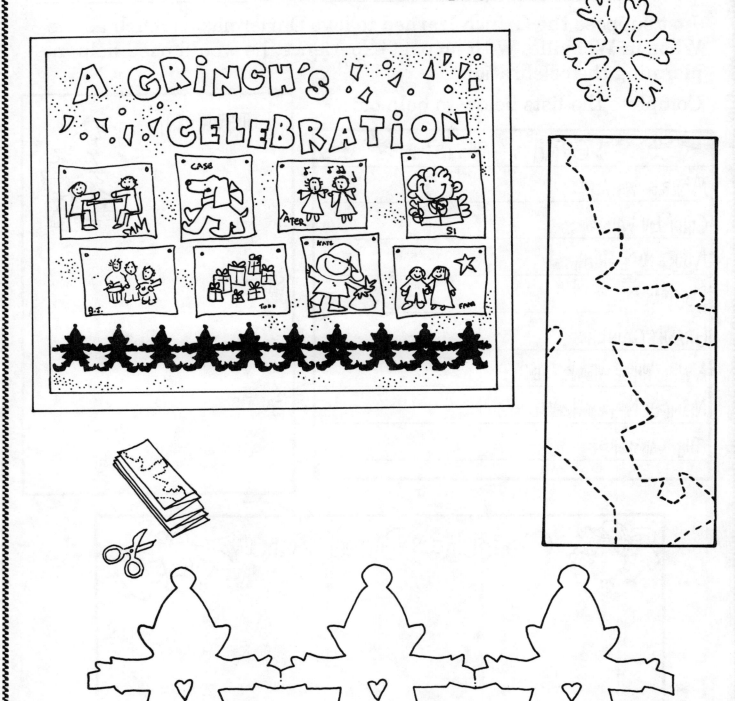

SUITED TO SIZE

Name _____ Date_____

Design a new Santa suit for the Grinch.

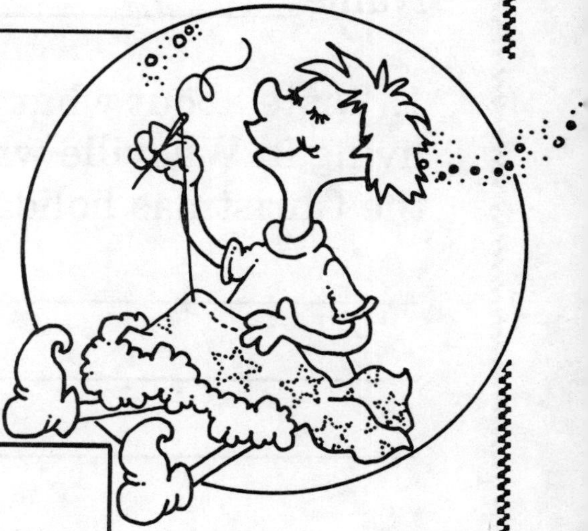

Coat

Trousers

Hat

Boots

Santa Grinch dressed to go.

WHAT, WHY, AND HOW

Name_____ Date _____

1. Write about what you would have done had you been a Who living in Whoville when you awoke on Christmas Day to find all the Christmas holiday goodies missing. _____

_____

_____

_____

_____

2. Write about why the Whos were able to sing and celebrate without presents, food, and even Christmas trees. _____

_____

_____

_____

_____

3. Write about how the Grinch must have felt when he was asked to carve the Christmas beast for the feast.

_____

_____

_____

_____

_____

WHO WORDS

Name_____ Date _____

The happy Whos of Whoville have fun with words just like you do.
They play word games, practice their spelling words, work word
puzzles, and do all kinds of fun things with words. Being the fun-
loving Whos they are, however, they love nonsense words best of all.

Help the Whos with their new dictionary by writing a sentence
using each of the "Who Words" below.

Who me_____

_____.

Who do _____

_____.

You who _____

_____.

Hi who _____

_____.

Ho who _____

_____.

They who _____

_____.

Do who _____

_____

WHAT IF...

Name _____ Date _____

What if the Grinch had not changed his mind about Christmas?
What if the Whos of Whoville had not had the Christmas goodies returned?
What if the Grinch had just stayed on his mountaintop to wait for another Christmas to come?

Draw pictures in the boxes below to show how the Grinch and the Whos would have spent Christmas Day.

WE WISH YOU A MERRY CHRISTMAS

We wish you a Merry Christmas;
We wish you a Merry Christmas;
We wish you a Merry Christmas
And a Happy New Year.

Name _____ Date_____

My Christmas wish for

my parents is _____

_____

my best friend is _____

_____

my teacher is _____

_____

the world is _____

VALENTINE'S DAY

A Time of Love
and Friendship,
Giving and Caring

TEACHER OVERVIEW

Wilfrid Gordon McDonald Partridge, written by Mem Fox and illustrated by Julie Vivas. Originally published in Australia by Omnibus Books in 1984; American edition by Kane/Midler Book Publishers, Brooklyn, New York, 1985.

THE AUTHOR

Mem Fox was born in Melbourne, Australia, but she spent much of her early life in Zimbabwe. She moved back to her native country as an adult. She now lives in Adelaide, Australia, with her husband and daughter. Mem teaches at a college there. She loves telling and writing stories for children and travels around the world sharing her wonderful talents with others.

THE ILLUSTRATOR

Julie Vivas is an Australian artist whose lovely book illustrations bring joy to children of all ages. For a while she lived in Spain, but she now lives with her husband and two daughters in Sydney, Australia.

THE STORY

Wilfrid Gordon McDonald Partridge is a heartwarming account of a small boy's successful attempt to help an elderly friend regain her lost memory. In his quest for understanding of "memory," this little boy receives sage advice from a bevy of older friends which he, in turn, translates into real items. Happily, the treasures he shares with Miss Nancy Alison Delacourt Cooper do serve to restore the lost memory. The real power of this tender little story, however, lies in the strength of friendship shared between two people of vastly differing ages and experiences.

WORDS TO KNOW

secrets	wonderful	*precious
remember	laughter	*favorite
gently	found	*surprising

*bonus (difficult) words

EXPLORING THE HOLIDAY

THE THEME: VALENTINE'S DAY: A Time Of Love And Friendship, Giving And Caring

The celebration of Valentine's Day actually began as Saint Valentine's Day. According to legend, somewhere around the third century, there really was a Saint Valentine who suffered and died for love. Many different stories have been told about the origin and history of this holiday, but all accounts seem to agree — Valentine's Day as we know it today is definitely a day set aside to celebrate love, friendship, giving, and caring.

On February 14, greetings are mailed or delivered by hand to convey "love messages" to parents, neighbors, friends, and lovers. In modern times, paper, lace, silk and satin hearts, flowers, chocolates, greeting cards, and fake and real jewels have been used to supplement the traditional handwritten notes associated with Valentine's Day. Some people even like to send anonymous greetings to keep the recipient wondering who sent them. Sometimes these anonymous notes are sent in the form of comics with hidden messages, but more often they carry messages for secret admirers or someone who just wants to add a note of mystery to a friend or relative's day.

No one seems to know for sure how the color red and the heart symbol became associated with Valentine's Day traditions. Whatever the reasons, red hearts accompany almost all Valentine's Day celebrations today. We do know for sure, however, that over the years Valentine's Day has become a time for people to express their love and concern for the special people in their lives.

Even more importantly, the observance of this day encourages a spirit of goodwill and respect for fellow human beings. Valentine's Day truly is a time of love, friendship, giving, and caring.

MOTIVATIONAL ACTIVITY

Use the unit cover page as a poster to create the setting for a celebration of Valentine's Day as a time of love and friendship, giving and caring. Discuss the history and meaning of Valentine's Day, and encourage students to share Valentine's Day insights and experiences.

Provide red construction paper and other art supplies, and ask students to create large valentines for a bulletin board display. Add letters, notes, slogans, and other valentine's messages to the board as the unit progresses.

SHARING THE BOOK

Read *Wilfrid Gordon McDonald Partridge* aloud in one sitting. Plan for plenty of time to share each illustrated page with the students, since the facial features and "personality poses" of the characters do much to enhance and extend the story's subtly presented plot. Discuss ways this boy "who wasn't very old either" demonstrated true traits of loving, giving, and sharing.

POINTS TO PONDER

1. Why did Wilfrid Gordon enjoy spending time with people living in the old people's home?

2. What are some things he might have learned from his older friends?

3. How do you think Miss Nancy would feel if Wilfrid Gordon and his family moved to another town?

4. Of all the things in the basket, which do you think Miss Nancy liked most? Why?

5. Which thing do you think Wilfrid Gordon treasured most? Why?

6. Both Wilfrid Gordon and Miss Nancy had four names. What would be your name if you could add enough names to your present name to have four?

SCIENCE – "Exploring Eggs"

Reread the two passages related to the fresh warm egg Wilfrid Gordon took from under the hen. Have students name animals other than chickens that lay eggs. List these animals on a chart and ask students to look for pictures in magazines to illustrate the chart. Discuss how baby animals are hatched from eggs, nests and nesting habits, and mothers' behavior with their young.

ART – "A Bird's Nest"

Distribute large sheets of drawing paper and crayons and ask students to draw pictures of the bird and its nest and eggs as they think Miss Nancy remembered them from her aunt's garden.

SOCIAL STUDIES/VALUING – "Treasures To Share"

Lead a class discussion related to aging and the elderly. Encourage students to describe older people they know and name things they enjoy doing with older people. Reread the pages and share again the illustrations of the things Wilfrid Gordon collected to share with Miss Nancy. Point out that each item was carefully selected with love, and ask students to discuss why he decided to share these particular things and why

and how they helped Miss Nancy regain her memory. Ask students to name things from their own "treasures" that they would have shared with Miss Nancy had they been in Wilfrid Gordon's place. Distribute copies of the "Treasures to Share" work sheet and ask students to complete according to directions. Add the finished product to the Valentine's Day bulletin board.

WRITING – "A Special Thank-You"

Reproduce and distribute copies of the "A Special Thank-You" work sheet and ask students to write a letter that Miss Nancy might have written to thank Wilfrid Gordon for helping her get her memory back.

MATH – "Math Memory"

Distribute copies of the "Math Memory" work sheet. Set the stage for the math memory game by telling students Wilfrid Gordon might have enjoyed sharpening his memory by completing this work sheet and sharing it as a game with one of his elderly friends. After the work sheet is completed, ask students to make up a "Math Memory" work sheet of their own for a friend to complete.

LANGUAGE EXTENSION –
"Making and Using Puppets"

Discuss the puppet in Wilfrid Gordon's basket and how it made Miss Nancy smile as it brought back memories of her sister's laughter. Talk about different kinds of puppets and the ways they can be used to make people smile. Reproduce and distribute copies of the "People Puppets" page for students to complete and cut out. Have students work in groups to make up and present plays to bring smiles to people's faces.

FIELD TRIP

Visit a home for the elderly if possible and present the plays.

LITERATURE BONUS

Place a copy of *Chickens Aren't The Only Ones* on the free-reading table. Students will love and learn from the fanciful illustrations of the many exotic creatures that hatch their young from eggs.

CULMINATING ACTIVITY –
"A Time Of Love And Friendship, Giving And Caring"

Wilfrid Gordon's elderly friends would certainly have loved strings of happy hearts hanging from their doors, windows, and ceilings.

Divide the students into small groups. Give each group a copy of the "Happy Hearts" work sheet. Provide art supplies necessary for completing the activity. Allow groups to work independently to follow the directions to make "Happy Hearts" mobiles.

Reassemble the total group to share and evaluate the completed mobiles. If possible, deliver the completed mobiles to a hospital or nursing home. If not, hang them around the classroom as a reminder that Valentine's Day is a time of love and friendship, giving and caring.

TREASURES TO SHARE

Name_____ Date _____

Treasures do not always come from stores, and many cannot be bought for money.

Fill this treasure chest with words and pictures to show six treasures that you would share with an older friend.

A SPECIAL THANK-YOU

Name _____ Date _____

Write a thank-you letter that Miss Nancy might have written to thank Wilfrid Gordon for helping her get her memory back.

Vocabulary:

secrets	wonderful	gently
remember	laughter	favorite
precious	found	surprising

MATH MEMORY

Name_____ Date_____

Complete the patterns by writing the appropriate number in each heart.

5 ♡   15 ♡   ♡   30 ♡

10 ♡   ♡ 40   ♡   ♡ 70

15 ♡   ♡ 18   19 ♡   ♡

22 ♡   26 ♡   ♡   32 ♡

20 ♡   ♡ 80   ♡ 120   ♡

33 ♡   39 ♡   45 48 ♡

4 ♡   12 ♡   ♡   24 ♡

PEOPLE PUPPETS

Name _____ Date _____

Color and cut out the puppets.
Use them to bring a smile to someone's face.

HAPPY HEARTS

Name_____ Date _____

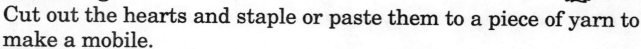

Use crayons, markers, or paints to decorate the hearts.
Write a word or phrase on each heart to show that
Valentine's Day is a time of love and friendship, giving
and caring.
Cut out the hearts and staple or paste them to a piece of yarn to
make a mobile.
Use your imagination to make the mobile as creative as possible.

SAINT PATRICK'S DAY

A Time for Magic, Mystery & Malarkey

TEACHER OVERVIEW

The Leprechaun's Story, written by Richard Kennedy and illustrated by Marcia Sewall. Published by E.P. Dutton, New York, 1979.

THE AUTHOR

Richard Kennedy is equally well-acclaimed as a storyteller and author. He is known for his sense of humor, respect for leprechauns, and skeptical view of the world. His home is in Newport on the coast of Oregon. Other books include *The Porcelain Man*, *The Blue Stone*, and *The Rise And Fall Of Ben Gizzard*.

THE ILLUSTRATOR

Marcia Sewall is an accomplished artist working in Boston. She is the illustrator of Edward Lear's *The Nutcracker And The Sugartongs*, which was established as a New York Times best illustrated book; *The Wee, Wee Mannie And The Big, Big Coo*; and *Master Of All Masters*. She has illustrated other books written by Richard Kennedy.

THE STORY

This magical story with delightful pen and ink drawings portrays a tradesman's determination to make his fortune and a leprechaun's equal determination to keep his gold. The story is based on the Irish legend that when you find a leprechaun and keep your eyes on him, he must take you to his pot of gold. If your eyes wander, the leprechaun and the treasure disappear. The greedy tradesman refuses to take his eyes off the leprechaun in spite of dangers described by the mysterious little man. The leprechaun's trickery finally wins out as the author and artist creatively unravel this too-tragic-to-be-true yarn.

WORDS TO KNOW

leprechaun	skiff	charity	*tradesman
profit	canyon	overcome	*hedgerow
greedy	aye	attend	*cobbling
wits	heathen	bonny	*plight
imp	grubs	lass	
feeble	bawled		

*bonus (difficult) words

EXPLORING THE HOLIDAY

THE THEME:
SAINT PATRICK'S DAY –
A Time For Magic, Mystery, And Malarkey

Even though Saint Patrick's Day honors Saint Patrick as the patron saint of Ireland, people from many different backgrounds look forward to celebrating this special day. On March 17 each year, festive dinners, dances, parades, and jolly sing-alongs are enjoyed by young and old around the globe. People wear green shamrocks, whistle Irish tunes, dance Irish jigs, and wave Irish flags.

Interestingly enough, Saint Patrick was born and reared in Scotland, not Ireland. As a very young man, he was captured by pirates and taken to Ireland, where people were then worshipping idols. He was sold as a slave and escaped after six years. He then studied to become a priest in order to teach the Irish people about the God he believed in.

Legend has it that during this teaching priesthood, he managed to mysteriously banish all the snakes from Ireland. To this day the Irish people say there is not a snake to be found in all of Ireland.

In modern times, Saint Patrick's Day has become a day for merrymaking and celebrations flavored with magic, mystery, and malarkey.

MOTIVATIONAL ACTIVITY

Discuss Saint Patrick's Day and associated symbols such as the color green, shamrocks, leprechauns, and the legend of the pot of gold at the rainbow's end. Locate Ireland on a world map and find and discuss the neighboring countries.

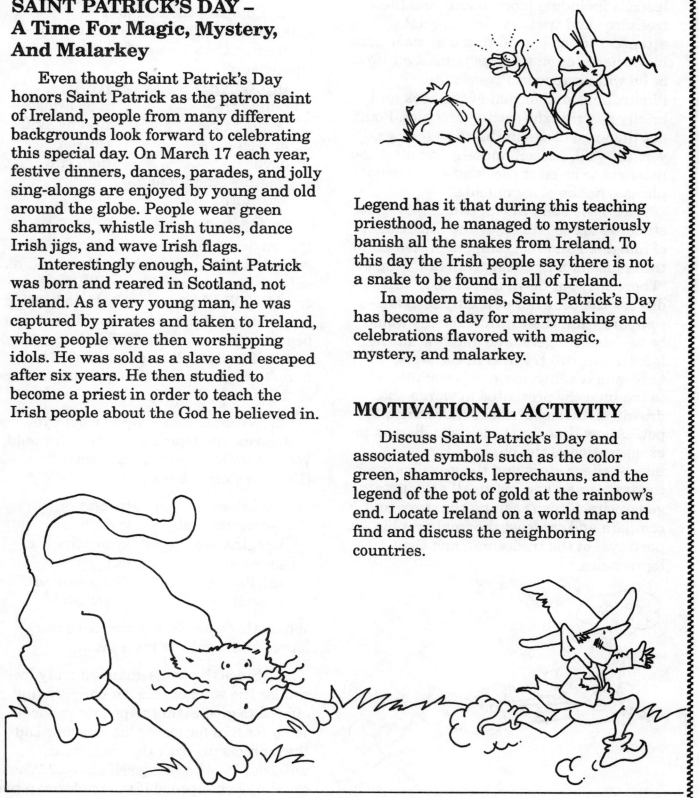

SHARING THE BOOK

Before reading the book, discuss Irish legends including leprechauns and their treasures and trickery. Give special attention to the legend that one must keep his or her eyes on a leprechaun at all times or he will disappear. Present the illustrations and format of the book and briefly describe the setting and plot. Point out the word usage in the story (i.e., ye, yer, 'tis, ye'll, herself, meself) and alert the listeners to be on the lookout for unusual phrases as the story unfolds.

Read the story aloud, pausing to allow students to see and enjoy the illustrations of imagined and real dangers presented to the tradesman by the leprechaun. Stop at, "There they sat down and rested," to discuss the behavior of the tradesman, compare what their own reactions would be to these dangers, and guess what the leprechaun will try next in the story. Continue reading, giving special attention to the imagery presented in words and drawings, through "...let's leave them the pot!" Allow time for students to discuss the exaggeration of the plight of the make-believe story and the greediness of the tradesman and his small attempt at generosity. Finish reading the story, and compare and contrast the final graphic portrayal of the tradesman and the leprechaun.

POINTS TO PONDER

1. Compare the real and make-believe effects used to cause the tradesman to look away from the leprechaun.

IMAGINED	REAL
falling tree	rope bridge
leaping tiger	tipping skiff
lass on horse	canyon
devil	high cliff
"picture" the woman	
sad story	

2. Retell the exaggerated troubles of the tragic woman to emphasize the leprechaun's clever trickery. Do you think only one person could have all these troubles? Would you have believed such a tragic story? If not, when would you have begun to get suspicious? Why do you think the tradesman believed the tale? If he hadn't, would it have changed the outcome of the story?

3. Which of these words would you use to describe the leprechaun? Which would you use to describe the tradesman? (Explain your choices.)

trickster	careful
determined	greedy
imaginative	sympathetic
generous	hungry
intelligent	disappointed
winner	unselfish

Which three words describe both the leprechaun **and** the tradesman?

4. Since the tradesman did truly feel sad for the woman and her children and offered to give them the pot, do you feel sorry for him for losing his fortune? Did the leprechaun trick the tradesman unfairly? Was he being selfish, too? What could have happened if the tradesman had agreed to share?

CURRICULUM INTEGRATION

MATH – "Number Memory Mystery"

As a total group, refer to the book to find the number of imaginary and the number of real experiences given to the tradesman by the leprechaun. Use these figures to practice writing number sentences.
Example:

_____ + ____ = _____
Imagined plus Real equals Total Experiences

_____ + _____ = _____
  I   R   T

_____ - _____ = _____
  T   R   I

_____ - _____ = _____
  T   R   I

Ask students to create other problems. Reproduce, distribute, and provide time for completing the "Number Memory Mystery" work sheet.

SCIENCE – "Irish Gardening"

Use reference materials to find information about grubs, the terrain of Ireland, and what crops could be growing in the woman's Irish garden.

SOCIAL STUDIES – "Excuses, Excuses"

The tradesman used factual knowledge as well as rationalization to keep his eyes on the leprechaun. He knew not to turn around for an imaginary falling tree, leaping tiger, bonny lass on a horse, or devil. He knew he could "picture" in his mind the tragic woman without closing his eyes. He knew he could chance dangers, but he had to search for reasons not to be sorry enough for the woman to give her the gold. Use these examples to discuss how the tradesman was trying to excuse his greed.

1. "...it's lucky he is to be alive, and a horse is always valuable."
2. "...the poor family was left with a cow..."
3. "...they have a dog..."
4. "There's no understanding it."
5. "...leave them the pot!"

Personalize this discussion to include rationalization possibilities in the classroom. Sample excuses used to avoid getting into trouble or feeling guilty are:

• "I didn't do my math, but I know my spelling words."
• "She hit me first."
• "...but I found it on the floor..."
• "I had lots of paper last week."
• "My mother always puts it in my backpack."

Encourage students to supply other examples.

ART – "Picture It"

Reproduce and distribute the "Picture It…" drawing sheet. Instruct the students to "picture" in their minds one of the following story lines not illustrated in the book and then to "picture it" on the paper.

• Then the man went to walking into a well…

• …the poor woman is out digging grubs…

• Yer own self will soon have a whole pot of gold.

• …a hut that's no more than a patch on the ground…

Allow time for discussing the pictures.

COOPERATIVE LEARNING – "In Other Words"

Compile a class book of descriptive phrases often used in literature or conversation. Allow the students to work in groups of four to define and illustrate the following phrases:

- fat as a pig
- mind went blank
- talked a blue streak
- hid her face
- busy as a bee
- took his word
- quiet as a mouse
- thin as a rail
- could sleep forever
- smart as a whip
- hungry as a horse
- sight unseen
- mountain out of a molehill

LANGUAGE – "Compare And Contrast"

Compare and contrast the following concepts and how they relate to the story:

Real vs. imaginary

Greed vs. sharing

Fair vs. unfair

Smart vs. foolish

Honest vs. trickery

Discuss ways the little leprechaun's story presented magic, mystery, and malarkey to entertain and spellbind the reader.

CULMINATING ACTIVITY – "A Time For Magic, Mystery, And Malarkey"

Lead a discussion of leprechauns and imaginary creatures associated with the magic, mystery, and malarkey of Saint Patrick's Day. Distribute copies of the "If I Met A Leprechaun" work sheet, and ask students to stretch their imaginations to complete the activity.

NUMBER MEMORY MYSTERY

Name_____ Date_____

Test your memory by answering the questions to complete the mystery sentences. If you need help, refer to the code box.

How many children did the tragic woman have?

$\overline{\text{I}}$

How many pots would the tradesman give away?

$\overline{\text{T}}$

How many legs did the poor dog have?

$\overline{\text{D}}$

How many real dangers did the tradesman have?

$\overline{\text{Y}}$

What was the age of the oldest child?

$\overline{\text{R}}$

What was the total number of tricks tried?

$\overline{\text{K}}$

How many cows and horses were in the story?

$\overline{\text{C}}$

How many characters were in the story?

$\overline{\text{E}}$

How many imagined efforts were tried?

$\overline{\text{S}}$

How did the leprechaun get the tradesman to cover his __ __ __ __ ?

$\overline{9}\ \overline{4}\ \overline{9}\ \overline{6}$

He __ __ __ __ __ __ __ him!

$\overline{1}\ \overline{8}\ \overline{5}\ \overline{2}\ \overline{10}\ \overline{9}\ \overline{3}$

I = 5	Y = 4	C = 2
T = 1	R = 8	E = 9
D = 3	K = 10	S = 6

PICTURE IT...

Name _____ Date _____

Story line to picture: _____

_____

_____

_____

IF I MET A LEPRECHAUN

Name _____ Date _____

If I met a leprechaun on the way to school, this is what I would say to him _____

_____

_____

_____

_____

_____

This is what I would do _____

_____

_____

_____

_____

_____

And this is what would happen next _____

_____

_____

_____

_____

_____

CELEBRATE WILDLIFE!

A Time To Treasure Our Natural Resources

TEACHER OVERVIEW

Faint Frogs Feeling Feverish by Lilian Obligado, Viking Press, New York, 1983.

THE AUTHOR

Lilian Obligado is the daughter of an author/editor and the granddaughter of a famous poet. She was born and raised in Argentina with lots of books, children, dogs, cats, chickens, geese, and hundreds of green parrots. She likes to write about things she sees around her. She has written only a few books herself but has illustrated over 50 children's books for other authors. She has homes in New York, Paris, and Switzerland.

THE STORY

Faint Frogs Feeling Feverish is an ABC collection of "amazingly alliterative animal tongue twisters," alias big, fun words! The charming and challenging alphabet book, which introduces readers to dozens of entertaining, energetic, (and some endangered) species, also sparks enthusiastic investigation of animal life both rare and familiar to young children. The "terrifically tantalizing tongue twisters" make it all great sport!

WORDS TO KNOW ABOUT WILDLIFE CONSERVATION

conservation – the careful use and protection of natural resources
development – the building up of an area with new farms, homes, or businesses
endanger – to put into a dangerous position
extinct – no longer living or existing
refuge – an area where animals can live safely from danger
rare – not found, seen, or happening very often

ANIMALS YOU MAY NOT KNOW

armadillo	boar	ferret	*auk
iguana	jerboa	kiwi	*aardvark
macaw	mongoose	platypus	*xemo
sole	toucan	urial	*xiphias
uakari	vole	wombat	
alpaca		yak	

*bonus (difficult) words

88

THE THEME: CELEBRATE WILDLIFE – A Time To Treasure Our Natural Resources

People in many countries have set aside special days of the year to celebrate some of their best friends – their friends in the animal world.

Our planet Earth was planned with a balance of human beings, plants, and animals in mind. But people can be Earth's best friends or worst enemies. People are not always thoughtful of plant and animal life. They often use animal resources for their own selfish purposes. Sometimes they kill animals just for fun or to get their furs. They burn or clear forests, destroying animal homes, and build cities on land that animals need for space to roam and find food. Even when they don't intend to, people poison air and water with fertilizers and insecticides that kill fish and small animals.

But some people who are very concerned about Earth's wildlife resources have planned special days and events to remind all of us how to enjoy and protect our wildlife. These days are not the same in all parts of the world, but wherever they are observed, they are a celebration of animal life and an effort to make all human beings aware of the special needs of some of Earth's most interesting and treasured creatures.

MOTIVATIONAL ACTIVITY

Use the cover page as a poster or bulletin board to introduce the theme of wildlife conservation – a celebration of animal life. Fill the classroom with books and pictures about animals, and set aside special times for movies, slides, and videos about animal life. Allow students to bring small, caged animals to the classroom for observation. (You might even invite a student collection of stuffed animals. See how many different kinds of animals are represented!) A field trip to a zoo or animal museum would be a delightful plus, but if that is impossible, at least have an afternoon tea party and serve animal crackers!

SHARING THE BOOK

Faint Frogs Feeling Feverish is a book bursting with big, fun words. Children of all ages will love the amusing illustrations, and for this reason the book needs to be shared slowly, in detail, and in as large a format as possible. Reading it to small groups is an excellent idea. Students need to be able to study the pictures as their tongues struggle with the "twisters."

Read each phrase slowly and point to its matching illustration. Take time to enjoy the picture; then say the phrase again and allow students to repeat it one or more times. (Sometimes they'll love trying to say it fast or taking turns saying it individually.) Younger students may enjoy imitating some of the actions or animal sounds.

Older or abler students can digest the book in one sitting. With younger students, two or more sittings will be preferable. When the entire first reading is complete, make the book available for students to peruse and enjoy on their own.

CURRICULUM INTEGRATION

SCIENCE – "Nurse Nightingale"

Reproduce and distribute to each student one copy of the "Nurse Nightingale" work sheet. Encourage and assist them in following directions to read and chart temperatures of the ailing animals.

MATH – "Math Menagerie"

Distribute one copy of the "Math Menagerie" work sheet to each student. After explaining written instructions, encourage students to complete the work sheet independently.

WRITING – "Llama Laughing," "Toad Telling Tall Tales"

Reproduce copies of the "Llama Laughing" and "Toad Telling Tall Tales" work sheets and let students choose one or both as creative writing assignments. Share the finished products!

ENRICHMENT – "Hares And Hounds"

Choose 3-5 students to be hares, and assign the remainder of the class to be hounds. The hares will need sliced raw potatoes, carrots, or squash in resealable plastic bags and a large bag of dry beans. This is an outdoor game. Hares get a 5 - 10 minute start. They drop a piece of sliced vegetable about every 20 yards and drop two or three beans on the ground at small intervals between the sliced veggies. They make a trail as long and as complicated as possible. At or near the end of the trail, they all hide. The hounds then follow the trail and try to find the hares. They pick up the clues as they go along. Score 1 point for each veggie slice and 2 points for each bean. Play the game as many times as possible or until everyone has had a chance to be a hare!

ART – "Blob Art"

Provide large sheets of black and white construction paper, brightly colored tempera paints, and small squeeze bottles. Allow each student to choose black or white paper and several bright colors of paint. Using the squeeze bottles, the artist should place large blobs of several different colors on his or her white or black background. The blobs should be allowed to dry; then several additional blobs may be added. Encourage students to use their blob-painting skills to create an imaginative wildlife creature for whom they make up a name and some wild stories!

LANGUAGE/MUSIC ENRICHMENT – "Lobster Language"

Provide one "Lobster Language" work sheet for each student. Ask students to follow directions to decode the hidden message and complete the song. When all have finished, sing together the simple song they have discovered.

CULMINATING ACTIVITY – "A Time To Treasure Our Natural Resources"

Make copies of the list of endangered species. Ask each student to choose one animal to investigate. (You might star on the list one animal representing each letter of the alphabet and encourage students to choose those animals so that when the project is finished, you will have a complete alphabet of endangered animals to display in the classroom.) Allow plenty of research time and assistance in the library or classroom. Ask students to locate a picture and make a list of at least five important facts related to their animal. Pictures may be drawn, copied, or cut from magazines. Mount along with the important facts on a sheet of colored construction paper. Display in ABC order.

NURSE NIGHTINGALE

Name _____ Date_____

Nurse Nightingale is taking temperatures to see who's sick.
One of her patients is faking.
Which one is it?

Color a block on the chart for each degree of temperature.

	AILING ALPACA	BELLYACHE BEAR	FAINT FROG	DIZZY DINOSAUR	SNEEZING SQUIRREL
104					
103					
102					
101					
100					
99					
98.6					

Normal

MATH MENAGERIE

Name _____ Date _____

These math problems are missing some facts. Write a number in each blank space. Then solve each problem.

Driving Deer drove _____ miles yesterday and _____ miles today. How many miles did he drive?

_____

Cooking Cat has used _____ pounds of sugar, _____ pounds of flour, and _____ pounds of raisins. How many pounds of food has she used to cook? _____

Beaver is building a _____ foot boat. He has a board that is too long for the boat. It is _____ "too long." How much too long is it? _____

Monkey measured Mr. Moose. He is _____ inches tall. Mrs. Moose is _____ inches tall. Which moose is shorter? How many inches shorter? _____

Shelly Seal wants you to make up your very own problem about her shell shop. Use the space provided. Ask a friend to solve your problem.

LLAMA LAUGHING

Name _____ Date_____

Llama is "cracking up" over his own funny jokes.
Use the space below to make up two funny animal jokes that Llama may have told.
Try them on your friends.

94

TOAD TELLING TALL TALES

Name _____ Date _____

Pretend you are Toad. You are telling tall tales to Termite. One is silly. One is scary.
Write your tall tales! Remember ... they are just pretend!

Silly Tall Tale

Scary Tall Tale

LOBSTER LANGUAGE

Name _____ Date _____

Did you know that lobsters speak sea language?
It is a secret, salty language.
See if you can use the code to discover what Lobster is saying.

The code key:

sailboat	A	snail	I	octopus	O	crab	U
star	D	life ring	M	scallop	P	ferry	Y
fish	E	eel	N	seaweed	T		

A SELECT LIST OF 200 ENDANGERED SPECIES WORLDWIDE

For a complete list, write the U.S. Fish and Wildlife Service, Publications Unit, Washington, D.C. 20240. (The complete list includes nearly 800 animals.)

AFRICA

Mammals

Antelope, giant sable
Aye-aye
Bontebok
Cheetah
Chimpanzees
Deer, Barbary
Eland, western giant
Elephant, African
Gazelles (7 species)
Gorillas
Hyena, brown
Lemurs
Leopard
Manatee, West African
Mandrill
Monkeys (7 species)
Rhinoceros
Zebra, Grevy's
Zebra, mountain

Birds

Ostrich, West African
Rockfowl, white-necked

Reptiles

Crocodile (4 species)
Tortoise, radiated
Turtle, geometric

Amphibians

Toad, Cameroon

ARCTIC REGION

Mammals

Bear, brown
Bear, polar

ASIA

Mammals

Babirusa
Banteng
Bear, brown
Camel, Bactrian
Cat, leopard
Cat, marbled
Deer, Father David's
Deer, musk
Deer, swamp
Elephant, Asian
Gazelle, Arabian
Gazelle, sand
Gibbons
Horse, Przewalski's
Hyena, Barbary
Langur (9 species)
Leopard
Leopard, clouded
Leopard, snow
Lion, Asiatic
Macaque, lion-tailed
Orangutan
Oryx, Arabian
Rhinoceros (3 species)
Seledang (guar)
Siamang

Stag, Kashmir
Tiger
Yak, wild

Birds

Crane, black-necked
Crane, hooded
Crane, Japanese
Crane, Siberian white
Crane, white-naped
Eagle, Philippine monkey-eating
Egret, Chinese
Hornbill, helmeted
Ibis, Japanese crested
Ostrich, Arabian
Owl, giant scops
Pheasants (14 species)

Reptiles

Alligator, Chinese
Crocodile (5 species)
Gavial
Monitor (3 species)
Python, Indian

Amphibians

Salamander, Chinese giant
Salamander, Japanese giant

Fish

Ala Balik (trout)
Catfish, giant
Nekogigi (catfish)

AUSTRALIA AND NEW ZEALAND

Mammals

Bandicoot (3 species)
Kangaroo, eastern gray
Kangaroo, red
Kangaroo, western gray
Rat, Kangaroo (5 species)

Birds

Parakeet, hooded
Parrot, Australian
Thrush, New Zealand

Reptiles

Crocodile, saltwater
Tuatara

EUROPE

Mammals

Bear, brown
Chamois, Apennine
Ibex, Pyrenean
Lynx, Spanish

Birds

Eagle, Spanish imperial
Gull, Audouin's

HAWAIIAN ISLANDS

Birds

Coot, Hawaiian

Duck, Hawaiian
Duck, Laysan
Gallinule, Hawaiian
Goose, Hawaiian (Nene)
Honeycreeper (9 species)
Hawk, Hawaiian
Stilt, Hawaiian

NORTH AMERICA AND CENTRAL AMERICA

Mammals

Bat, gray
Bat, Indiana
Bear, grizzly
Bison, wood
Bobcat, Mexican
Caribou, woodland
Cougar, eastern
Deer, Columbian white-tailed
Deer, key
Ferret, black-footed
Fox, northern swift
Jaguarundi
Manatee, West Indian
Mouse, salt marsh harvest
Otter, southern sea
Panther, Florida
Prairie dog, Mexican
Pronghorn, Sonoran
Wolf, gray (except Alaska)
Wolf, red

Birds

Condor, California
Crane, whooping
Curlew, Eskimo
Eagle, Greenland white-tailed
Eagle, bald
Falcon, peregrine
Goose, Aleutian Canada
Kite, Everglade
Parrot, Cuban
Parrot, Imperial
Parrot, Puerto Rican
Pelican, brown
Prairie chicken, Attwater's greater
Quetzal, resplendent
Sparrow, dusky seaside
Warbler, Bachman's
Warbler, Kirtland's
Woodpecker, imperial
Woodpecker, ivory-billed

Reptiles

Alligator, American
Boa (4 species)
Chuckwalla, San Esteban Island
Crocodile, American
Crocodile, Cuban
Crocodile, Morelet's
Iguana (13 species)
Lizard, blunt-nosed leopard
Snake, eastern indigo
Snake, San Francisco garter
Tortoise, desert

Turtle, aquatic box

Amphibians

Salamander, Santa Cruz
Salamander, Texas blind
Toad, Houston
Treefrog, pine barrens

Fish

Chub (6 species)
Darter (8 species)
Pike, blue
Pupfish (5 species)
Sturgeon, short-nose
Trout (6 species)

Invertebrates

Snails (9 species)
Mussels (20 species)
Butterflies (10 species)

OCEANIC

Mammals

Seal, Caribbean monk
Seal, Hawaiian
Seal, Mediterranean
Whales (8 species)

Reptiles

Turtles, sea (6 species)

SOUTH AMERICA

Mammals

Armadillo, giant
Bear, spectacled
Chinchilla
Deer, marsh
Deer, pampas
Jaguar
Manatee, Amazonian
Margay (also N.A.)
Marmoset, cotton-top
Monkey (7 species)
Ocelot (also N.A.)
Otter (3 species)
Sloth, Brazilian three-toed
Tamarin (3 species)
Tapir (3 species)
Vicuna
Wolf, maned

Birds

Condor, Andean
Eagle, harpy
Grebe, Atitlan
Hawk, Galapagos
Macaw (3 species)
Parakeet, ochre-marked
Parrot, red-spectacled
Penguin, Galapagos
Rhea, Darwin's

Reptiles

Caiman (3 species)
Crocodile, Orinoco
Tortoise, Galapagos

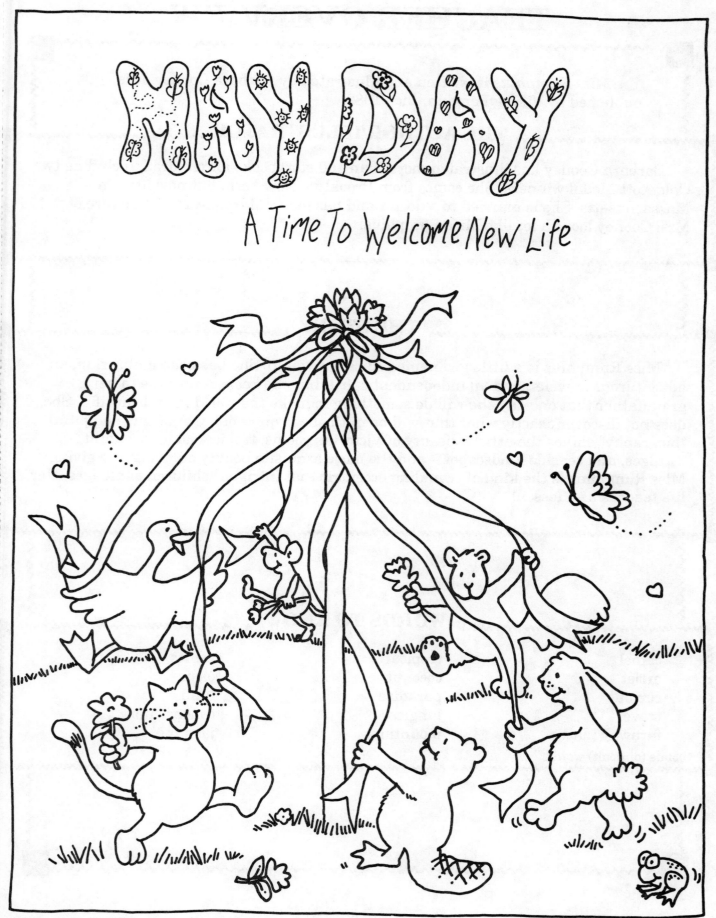

TEACHER OVERVIEW

Miss Rumphius is written and illustrated by Barbara Cooney. It is published by Viking Penguin, Inc., 1982.

THE AUTHOR/ILLUSTRATOR

Barbara Cooney has illustrated more than 100 storybooks for children, including two Caldecott Medal winners. She comes from Brooklyn, New York, but now lives in Massachusetts. She is married to a doctor and has four children. A recent picture of Mrs. Cooney looks a lot like Miss Rumphius!

THE STORY

Miss Rumphius is a little girl named Alice, grown up. She has been a librarian, an adventurous traveler, and an independent spirit, but she keeps a promise to her grandfather that one day she will do something to make the world more beautiful. She does not discover exactly what that will be until she is quite old. Out of this delightful "biography" shines the artistic beauty of Victorian rooms, tropical islands, quaint cottages, and seaside landscapes — and the more exquisite beauty of loving and giving. Miss Rumphius is the kind of twinkling eccentric that intrigues children of all ages. Her life teaches us a lesson!

WORDS TO KNOW

camel	tropical	deserts
artist	coconut	*oasis
curious	paradise	*lupine
travel	jungles	*conservatory
faraway places	mountains	*jasmine

*bonus (difficult) words

EXPLORING THE HOLIDAY

THE THEME: MAY DAY –
A Time To Welcome New Life

May Day is one of our oldest holidays. It began in ancient times when people worshipped many gods whom they honored on the first days of spring. They believed that as a result of May Day festivities, the sun would shine warmer and brighter, and flowers and plants would be more plentiful.

In the Western Hemisphere, we still celebrate May Day, not to please the gods, but to welcome the new life and colors of spring. In America, it is customary to gather flowers on May Day. Often, children make May baskets for their friends or for elderly people. They hang each basket on the doorknob of a friend or neighbor, ring the bell, and run away. Giving a May basket is like sending a secret valentine.

In 1907, New York school children began to hold May Day celebrations in the city parks. They danced about painted Maypoles and decorated them with ribbons or paper streamers and brightly colored balloons. In some places there is a May Queen who reigns over the festive events of the day. Hawaiian children make flower garlands called leis. They call the day Lei Day. Wherever May Day is celebrated, it is a joyous, happy festival of life.

MOTIVATIONAL ACTIVITY

Use the cover page as a poster or bulletin board to create a festive atmosphere for the celebration of May Day and the welcoming of fresh, new life and color of the spring season. Review the seasonal cycle and encourage students to point out environmental changes that mark the coming of spring. Talk about the new animal and plant life that emerges with warmer, wetter weather. Discuss the kinds of activities that make spring such a delightful season for human beings. If possible, gather live flowers and make May baskets or flower garlands. Share poems, songs, or pictures that celebrate the spring season.

SHARING THE BOOK

Make four large flash cards as pictured below.

Present the book by reading the title and looking at the picture on the cover. Talk about what kind of person Miss Rumphius might be. Let students share their ideas in single words and brief phrases. Explain that even though this story is only fictional, it is very similar to a biography – the story of a person's life.

Show the flash cards. Tell students that as you read the story, they should listen to see if they can recognize these four parts or "seasons" of Miss Rumphius's life. Then read the story, pausing to share each of the lovely illustrations.

 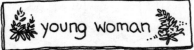

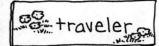 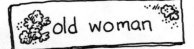

When the story has been read and enjoyed, talk about the character of Miss Rumphius. Was she as students expected? Ask different students to locate in the book at least one picture that represents Miss Rumphius at each stage of her life.

POINTS TO PONDER

1. What did Miss Rumphius do in her life that was most satisfying to her?

2. What are some other things that just one human being can do to make the world a more beautiful place?

3. How does the book *Miss Rumphius* fit with the idea of May Day and the celebration of spring? (love of nature, outdoor pleasures, giving to others)

CURRICULUM INTEGRATION

LANGUAGE/VOCABULARY – "Add A Petal"

Cut from colored construction paper at least six flower petals and one center (see page 108) for each student. Write the word "flowers" on the chalkboard. Ask students to brainstorm as a class to list words that describe flowers. Write the words on the board. Then pass out the flower parts. Ask students to write the word "flower" on the flower center. Then they must write one adjective for "flower" on each petal and attach it to the center. Words that appear in the original list on the chalkboard are not to be used! Make time for students to share their words. You may ask them to use two or more of the words on their petals to create a sentence about spring and write it on the back of their flower.

SOCIAL STUDIES/MATH – "The Oasis"

Reproduce a copy of the "The Oasis" work sheet for each student. Ask students to follow instructions to complete the page.

CREATIVE ARTS – "Tube Kites"

A tube kite is a perfect toy for enjoying spring winds! Supply for each student a piece of 9" x 12" white construction paper, tape, markers or crayons, colored crepe-paper streamers, and paper ribbon (three 10" pieces and one 24" piece). A stapler and paper punch should be available.

1. Use crayons and markers to decorate paper.

2. Roll into a tube and staple or fasten with tape.

3. Add long streamers.

4. Attach ribbon as shown at top.

5. Hold by long ribbon, and run into the wind.

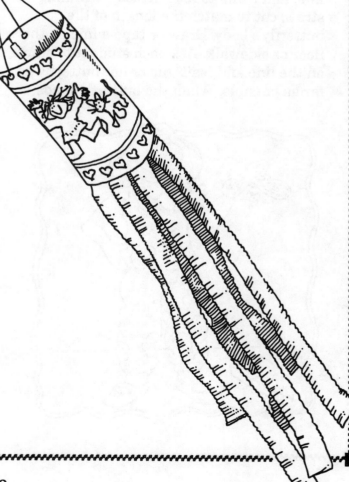

STUDY SKILLS/FOLLOWING DIRECTIONS – "Garden Snacks"

Divide students into small groups. Give each group a copy of the "Garden Snacks" work sheet. Provide appropriate ingredients and tools to complete recipes. Allow groups to work independently following written directions to make Cheese & Jelly Petals and Dirty Dessert. (Prepare the vanilla pudding and flowers for pots in advance. If real flowers are used, wrap stems in foil.)

MATH – "Butterfly Races"

Provide a copy of the butterfly pattern for each student. Ask students to color and cut out the butterfly. Fold on the dotted line, and using tape to attach a drinking straw, cut to match the length of the butterfly's body. Draw or tape a line on the floor or sidewalk. Ask each student to stand on the line and "sail" his or her butterfly as far as possible. When the butterfly lands, the student should use a tape measure to measure the distance the butterfly lands from the starting line. Each student has three tries. He or she records each distance in inches or centimeters and uses the farthest distance as his or her score. When all students have had a turn, scores should be recorded on a chart or chalkboard, and the class may work together to compute an average and median score and the total distance traveled by all butterflies!

SCIENCE – "See-Through Leaves"

Collect a variety of leaves. Discuss the variety of shapes, colors, and designs represented. Identify each leaf by name. Locate stems and veins.

Provide each student a copy of instructions for making "See-Through Leaves." Show a finished design, and be sure students have materials and understand how to proceed. (Assist students with ironing.)

Use transparent tape or fishing line to hang leaf designs in windows or against a lighted surface.

LITERATURE/WRITING EXTENSION – "Suppose-A-Boa"

Just for fun, read aloud and share the delightful illustrations of *Jimmy's Boa Bounces Back* (Trinka Hakes Nobel & Steven Kellogg. Dial Books, New York, 1984).

Discuss whether Miss Rumphius would have chosen to belong to this garden club had she lived in the neighborhood. Why or why not?

Talk about the progression of the story and how each catastrophic event builds on the previous one.

Then ask students to brainstorm together all the crazy events or mishappenings that could possibly take place at a big party where a boa gets loose. Write them on the board.

Make an optional assignment just for fun. Students may work alone or in pairs to use some of the suggestions on the board, trying their hand at creating a story that follows a pattern similar to *Jimmy's Boa Bounces Back*. These stories may be written or recorded. Allow those who wish to share their stories to do so.

ART BONUS – "Stuffed Boa"

Other students may enjoy using old nylon stockings stuffed with rags, tissue, or paper towels and bright-colored paints to create their own pet boa!

CULMINATING ACTIVITY – "A Time To Welcome New Life"

Ask students to locate library books about the story of May Day and the history of the Maypole. Each should write a brief, single-paragraph report on why people celebrate May Day. Enlist student assistance in planning an indoor or outdoor (preferable) Maypole dance complete with ribbons, balloons, and music. Make enough ribbons so that every student may have a turn at the Maypole dance. Involve students in construction of the Maypole and in choosing and making arrangements for the music accompaniment. Professional assistance in music and dance could be a great plus, but if not available, create your own homemade-style Maypole dances to celebrate and welcome new life.

THE OASIS

Name _____ Date_____

In the land of the Lotus-eater, Miss Rumphius hurt her back getting
off a camel. Perhaps her desert friends took her to an oasis. Deserts
are dry, dusty places.
Follow the directions to see if you can create a lovely oasis for
Miss Rumphius.

Directions

Draw
three
camels

Add
six
coconuts

Add
many
flowers

Draw
two
goats

Draw
four
people

Put
Miss Rumphius
in the picture

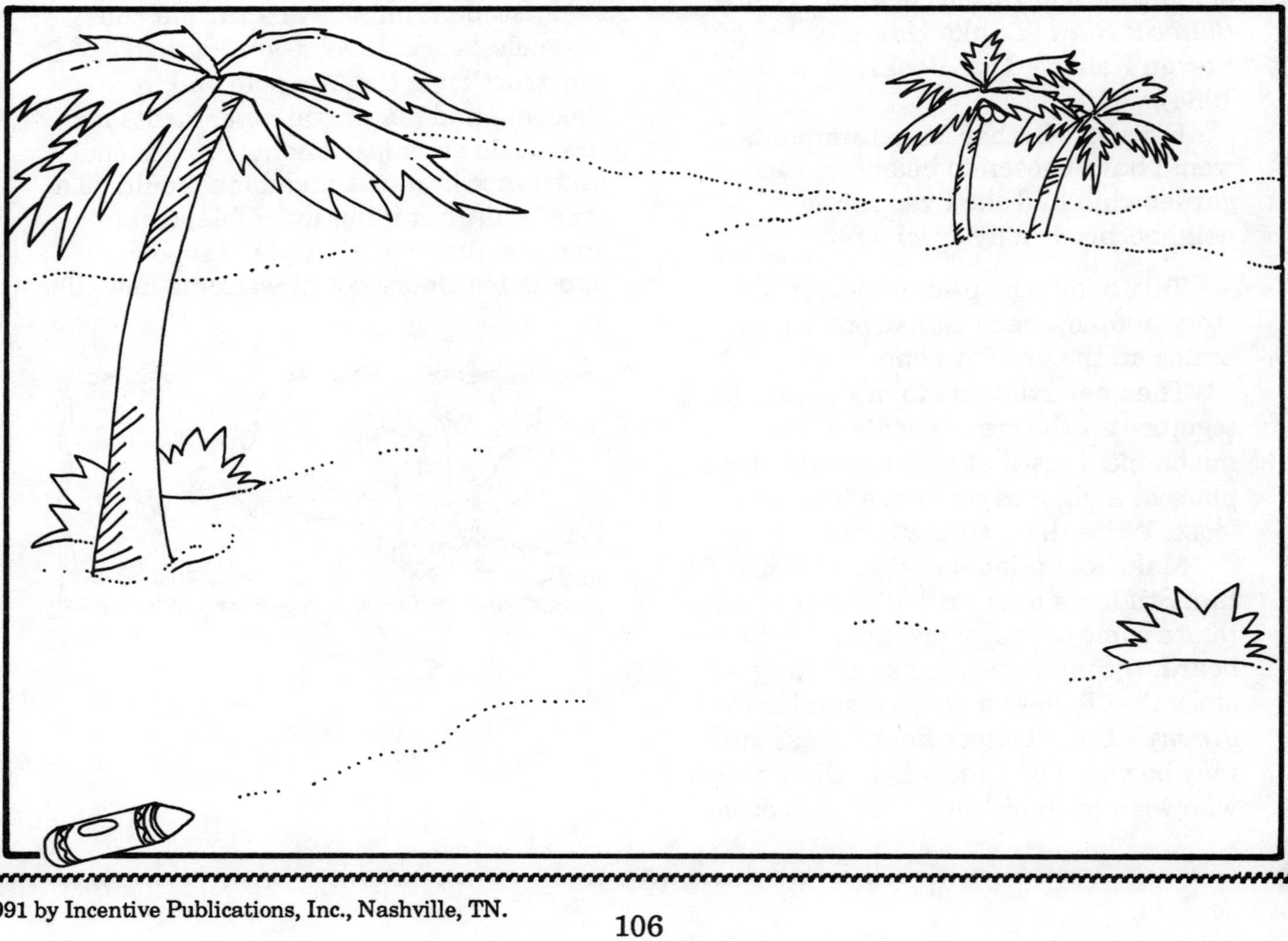

GARDEN SNACKS

To make **CHEESE & JELLY PETALS**

You need:

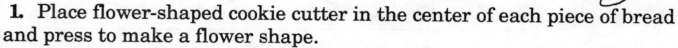

    thin white bread slices
    flower-shaped cookie cutters
    soft cream cheese
    jelly
    spoon
    knife
    food coloring to tint the cheese (optional)

1. Place flower-shaped cookie cutter in the center of each piece of bread and press to make a flower shape.
2. Use the knife to spread the flower with cheese.
3. Add a plop of jelly in the center!

To make **DIRTY DESSERT**

You need:

    tiny "flowerpots" (or paper cups)
    vanilla pudding
    chocolate cookies
    a resealable plastic bag
    a shoe
    real or pretend flowers
    spoons

1. Fill the flowerpots or paper cups half full with pudding.
2. Put the cookies in the bag. Lock shut.
3. Use the shoe to crush the cookies into crumbs.
4. Pour the cookie crumbs into the pot to look like dirt.
5. "Plant" a real or pretend flower in the center.

Serve with "Cheese & Jelly Petals"

Make place mats, set your table, and talk about the travels of Miss Rumphius while you munch on your GARDEN SNACKS.

"BUTTERFLY RACES" PATTERN

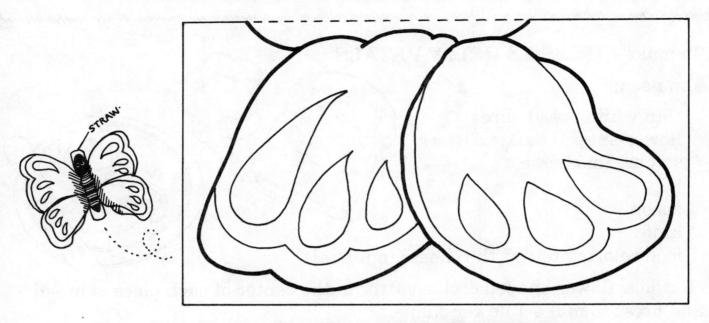

"ADD A PETAL" PATTERN

SEE-THROUGH LEAVES

What you need:

    2 pieces of newspaper
    2 pieces of waxed paper
    leaves or fern
    wax crayons
    dull knife or vegetable peeler
    iron

What to do:

1. Lay one piece of newspaper on a table.
2. Lay one piece of waxed paper on top of the newspaper.
3. Arrange leaves or fern on waxed paper.
4. Use a knife or peeler to scrape wax shavings over the leaves.
5. Cover the leaves and wax shavings with the second piece of waxed paper, matching corners of the first waxed paper exactly.
6. Cover with newspaper.
7. Press slowly and carefully with an iron to melt crayon and seal waxed paper.
8. Remove newspaper and hang up your see-through design.

SUMMER
A Time For Fun, Relaxation, and Travel

TEACHER OVERVIEW

The Relatives Came is written by Cynthia Rylant and illustrated by Stephen Gammel. It is published by Bradbury Press, an affiliate of MacMillan, Inc., New York, 1985.

THE AUTHOR

Cynthia Rylant has written several important children's picture books, a poetry book, a collection of short stories, and a novel. She and her family live in Akron, Ohio. (Hmmm ... maybe that's where the relatives lived!)

THE ILLUSTRATOR

Stephen Gammell has illustrated other award-winning books and has written some of his own. He lives in Minnesota. He has a beard and wears glasses.

THE STORY

A big, old station wagon overloaded with food, luggage, and a crowd of all shapes, sizes, and ages of people lumbers over mountain roads for a day and a night to unite two groups of relatives who live hundreds of miles apart. The visitors are welcomed with hugging and laughing, talking and making music, and the happy, contented sharing goes on for weeks as the relatives delight in just "being together."

WORDS TO KNOW

relatives	mountains	peaches
Virginia	hugging	*pajamas
station wagon	strawberries	*wrinkled
sandwich	grapes	*particular
summer	melons	*breathing

*bonus (difficult) words

© 1991 by Incentive Publications, Inc., Nashville, TN.

112

EXPLORING THE HOLIDAY

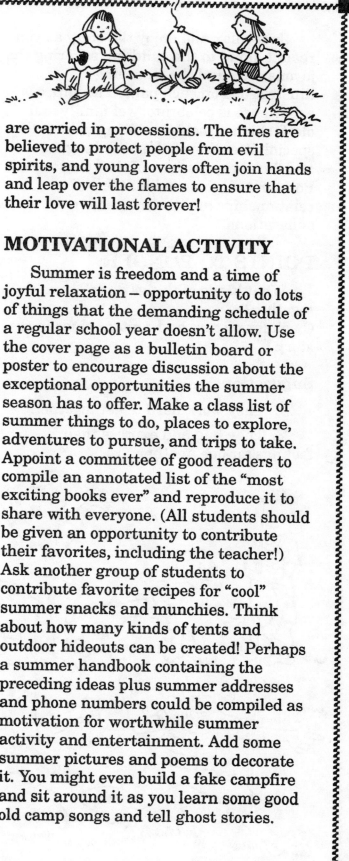

THE THEME: SUMMER –
A Time For Fun, Relaxation, And Travel

For most places in the world, summer is the time of long days and short nights. So it is a celebration of light ... with long hours to think, dream, and play.

Summer is the time when the earth's tilt means not only longer but stronger light. Across the earth's surface, it presents itself in different ways. In some places summer is scorching hot and dry. In others, a cool fog may hang overhead part of the day, then gradually burn away. Still other places are soggy with hot, heavy humid air so that when you go outside you feel almost as if someone has thrown a wet wool blanket over you. It seems hard to breathe.

In the far north, daylight stays almost 24 hours. It never gets really dark. There the plant life flourishes. (So do those ankle-biting mosquitoes!) Dry places remain a dull brownish-yellow, looking as if a broom has swept their color away. They await the fall and winter rains to become green again.

People of the world have celebrated summer in many ways. In Sweden, towns stage a battle between summer and winter. The winter team wears furs while the leader of summer is decorated with leaves and flowers. Summer always wins.

Midsummer's Eve, June 24th, the longest day of the year, is in many countries the most festive night of the year. Since ancient times, this night has been greeted around the world as a night of magic. To give the sun encouragement to stay high rather than sink lower in the sky, bonfires are lighted, and torches are carried in processions. The fires are believed to protect people from evil spirits, and young lovers often join hands and leap over the flames to ensure that their love will last forever!

MOTIVATIONAL ACTIVITY

Summer is freedom and a time of joyful relaxation – opportunity to do lots of things that the demanding schedule of a regular school year doesn't allow. Use the cover page as a bulletin board or poster to encourage discussion about the exceptional opportunities the summer season has to offer. Make a class list of summer things to do, places to explore, adventures to pursue, and trips to take. Appoint a committee of good readers to compile an annotated list of the "most exciting books ever" and reproduce it to share with everyone. (All students should be given an opportunity to contribute their favorites, including the teacher!) Ask another group of students to contribute favorite recipes for "cool" summer snacks and munchies. Think about how many kinds of tents and outdoor hideouts can be created! Perhaps a summer handbook containing the preceding ideas plus summer addresses and phone numbers could be compiled as motivation for worthwhile summer activity and entertainment. Add some summer pictures and poems to decorate it. You might even build a fake campfire and sit around it as you learn some good old camp songs and tell ghost stories.

SHARING THE BOOK

Just relax and enjoy the story as you read it aloud to the children, savoring the joyous copy and the charming illustrations on each page. The entire experience is celebratory of family and old-fashioned, self-sacrificing values. Pay special attention to the body language and facial expressions of the relatives. Point out all the combinations of relationships and the interaction of generations.

POINTS TO PONDER:

What kinds of things do relatives do together?
(Look for picture and content clues in the story.)

Suggestions:

1. They work hard to get together.
2. They hug and express their feelings for one another.
3. They eat together.
4. They share their belongings (food, beds, homes, etc.)
5. They talk to each other.
6. They work together.
7. They sing/play together.
8. They take pictures of each other.
9. They miss each other when they are gone away.
10. They think about each other.

As each suggestion is considered, find the copy or the illustration in the story that supports it.

Ask: How did the family feel when the relatives left?

Students may be encouraged to tell about special times they have spent with relatives.

CURRICULUM INTEGRATION

SOCIAL STUDIES – "Baggage Claim"

Make a copy of the "Baggage Claim" work sheet for each student. Examine with students the dedication pages of *The Relatives Came* and talk about the "personalities" of the various pieces of luggage pictured. Ask what kind of person might own each bag. Then ask students to identify the luggage pictured on the work sheet by filling in the luggage tag with a particularly appropriate name.

FOOD & FUN – "Tiny Icy Fruit Bowls"

Hollow out oranges or lemons, cutting off one end to make a cap. Fill each "bowl" with ice cream, yogurt, or fruit juice slush, and put the cap on and place it in the freezer. Thaw slightly before eating. Makes a yummy, healthy summer snack!

MATH – "How Far?"

Distribute one copy of the "How Far?" work sheet to each student. Let students work individually or in small groups to find the answers to the questions.

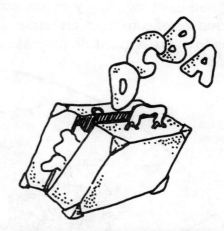

LANGUAGE ENRICHMENT – "I'm Going On A Trip!"

Play the age-old traditional travel game that tests ingenuity and memory. Students sit in a circle and pretend they are travelers. The first traveler says, "I am going on a trip, and I am going to take *(something beginning with the letter A, e.g., apple or aardvark)*. The second traveler says, "I am going on a trip, and I am going to take an apple and *(he or she adds an object that begins with the letter B)*. Each new traveler must repeat all objects mentioned before him or her and add a new one representing the next letter in the alphabet. The trip continues until travelers have included something representing each letter of the alphabet. ABC cards held by the players may help younger students remember. Older students may use double words such as *A – an ailing aardvark*, or *B – a baby buggy*.

ART/LITERATURE ENRICHMENT – "A Summer Poem Cycle"

Choose a group of children's poems related to summer and summer play. We suggest the classic poems of *A Child's Garden of Verses* by Robert Louis Stevenson, illustrated by Tasha Tudor (Rand McNally, Chicago, 1981), because of the lovely pictorial settings. Use white mural-size or poster paper to create a sun-shaped kaleidoscope arrangement on which illustrations for the poems can be drawn or copied. (Illustrations for the book may be copied by using an opaque or overhead projector, allowing students to do the tracing and coloring.) Copy or ask students with good penmanship to copy the poems on large squares of construction paper. Mount and coordinate them with the appropriate pictures to make a giant display as suggested below. Read them aloud often with the students.

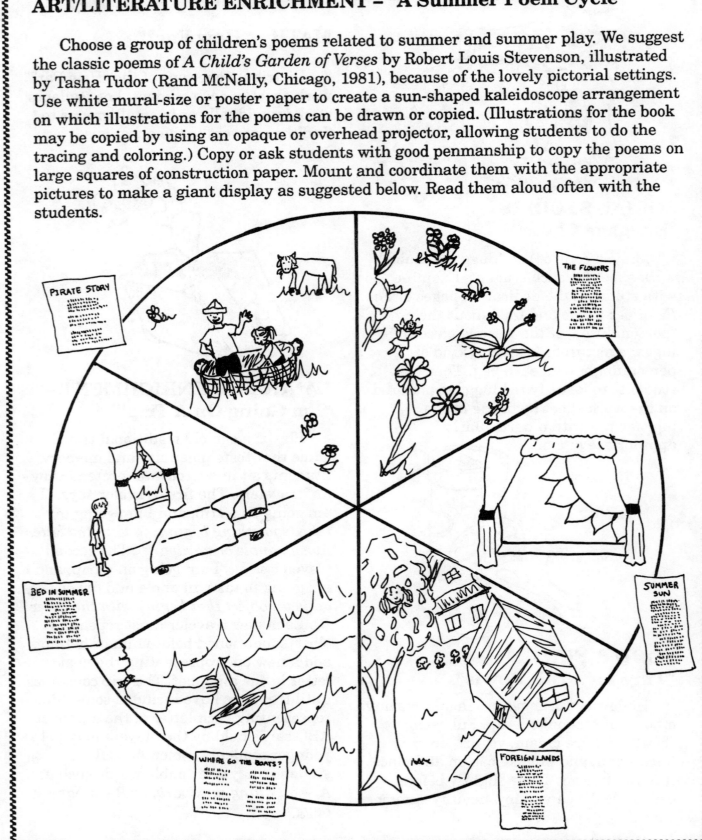

SCIENCE – "Body Clocks"

Make a body sunclock on the sidewalk or driveway. Mark an X in the center of the walk. Every hour, ask a member of the class to stand on the X and trace his or her shadow with chalk. Number the shadows. Everyone can see how ancient people told time by using the sun.

WRITING/ART – "Slide Show"

Cut overhead transparencies into four equal parts to make "slides." Distribute to each student six or eight slides and demonstrate how they may make frames from construction paper and tape them together on the backside. Ask each student to choose one of the following titles about which he or she will create his or her own brief slide show, drawing the pictures and writing the script he or she will read as he or she later "shows his or her slides" on the overhead projector.

- MY FAVORITE RELATIVE
- THE BEST TIME I EVER HAD WITH RELATIVES
- GOING TO VISIT THE RELATIVES
- WHEN THE RELATIVES CAME

CULMINATING ACTIVITY – "A Time For Fun, Relaxation, And Travel"

Reread the parts of the story that give hints about the location of the relatives' home. The book does not give a specific city or state. It does say the visitors came up from Virginia, over the mountains. They left at 4 a.m. and traveled all day and into the night. Look at a large road map of that section of the United States, and lead a discussion that encourages students to conjecture about the possible destination of the family's trip. Extend the activity to include discussion of family trips enjoyed by students, as well as trips they would like to take in the future. Locate on the map destinations mentioned, and trace the round trip routes.

BAGGAGE CLAIM

Name _____ Date _____

Look carefully at each piece of luggage.
What clues does it give you about its owner?
Decide what kind of person might own each piece.
Then make up a name that fits the perscnality of that person and
write it on the luggage tag.

HOW FAR?

Name _____ Date _____

Each •——• equals 5 miles.

How far does Aunt Jo have to travel to see Cousin Kat?_____

How far must Grandma travel to see Uncle Goober if she stops by Aunt Jo's?_____

If she stops by Cousin Kat's?_____

Which way is shorter?_____

Which two relatives live closest together?_____

How far would Uncle Goober travel if he visited all the other three relatives in this order – Cousin Kat, Grandma, Aunt Jo – then drove back home?_____

I CELEBRATE MY OWN SPECIAL DAYS!

A Time to Keep

Written by _____

TEACHER OVERVIEW

I'm In Charge Of Celebrations, written by Byrd Baylor and illustrated by Peter Parnall, is published by Charles Scribner's Sons, MacMillan Publishing Company, New York, 1986.

Tasha Tudor's *A Time To Keep* is published by Rand McNally and Company, New York, 1977.

THE AUTHORS/ILLUSTRATORS

Byrd Baylor is a Caldecott Honor Book Winner. She was born in Texas and now lives in Arizona. She is in love with the desert, and she really does create the kind of special, personal celebrations she writes about.

Peter Parnall has collaborated with Byrd Baylor on three Caldecott Honor books. He lives on a farm in Maine with his wife and children. People often say that he draws animals as the animals might see themselves. Look at the illustrations of the raven and quail. What do you think?

Tasha Tudor was born in Boston and grew up in Connecticut. She wrote her first book in 1938 and has written more than 40 books since that time. Her books have a special quality of "family" and traditional values about them. Many of them have a familiar New England flavor.

THE STORIES

I'M IN CHARGE OF CELEBRATIONS

"Last year I gave myself 108 celebrations — besides the ones that they close school for." This quote from the author provides just a glimpse into the purpose and profile of the story. Both whimsical and practical, the tale is an account of how and why the author creates extraordinary celebrations to mark ordinary, everyday events. To the adult reader, the book brings to mind the idea that all of us could benefit by utilizing this brilliant "unstressing" technique. For children, it can lead to the wonderful, early, life-changing discovery of the many delightful, positive, extraordinary moments in what often threatens to be a dull, humdrum world.

A TIME TO KEEP

"Time is an endless song," wrote William Butler Yeats. Tasha Tudor believed him and savored that time in one of the most cherishable books ever written for children — her own children. *A Time To Keep* is a book that commemorates the holidays of all our childhoods — the memories and the excitement that lead us through every year, always in anticipation of the next celebration. It is filled with the sights, sounds, smells, and delights of special family times together — times that are often sidetracked or forgotten in our fast-paced world. Children need to understand that there are always times to cherish — to "keep" — in their hearts, if no other place. The time spent sharing this book with children will be a "holiday" in itself!

THE THEME: I CELEBRATE MY OWN SPECIAL DAYS – A Time To Keep

Celebrations are not exclusively reserved for recognized holidays, birthdays, and world or social events. Sometimes they are very private, intimate affairs, observed only by one person – and often only in the most secret of secret places – the heart! Authors Byrd Baylor and Tasha Tudor lead a grand parade of magnificent possibilities and probabilities for celebrations – even the most unusual and unlikely occasions! They teach us that we can celebrate things like falling stars, green clouds, dust devils, rainbows, cousins, dolls, books, trees, or a chance meeting with a coyote! They show us how to do it with dances, games, feasts, pen and paper, candles, flowers, acorn teacups, races, contests, floating cakes and puppet shows, fireworks and drums, or just simple, quiet smiles and walks barefooted. They encourage us to be spinners of dreams and passionate lovers of extraordinary moments in the ordinary days of our lives. Time is to celebrate!

MOTIVATIONAL ACTIVITY

Reproduce the cover page of this unit and a set of the monthly pages at the end of the unit for each student. Show the covers of *I'm In Charge Of Celebrations* and *A Time To Keep*. Discuss the titles and allow students to conjecture about the themes and ideas that might be presented in the stories. Talk about the word "celebration." Ask students to suggest reasons and occasions for people to celebrate. Pass out copies of the cover page of the unit. Observe the illustrations in the border and let students identify the various celebrations they might represent. Explain to students that they will get an opportunity to create a medium for recording and cherishing their very own celebrations – their own special "times to keep!" They will use the cover page and the monthly pages to make a mini-notebook of celebrations to keep all year long. They should cut on the dotted lines to remove the title portion of the cover page to use as a booklet cover. The border illustrations may be cut, colored, and used as illustrations to be distributed throughout the pages of the book as students choose. To prepare the booklet pages, students cut on the dotted lines, punch at the solid dots, and then fasten cover and pages together by threading ribbon or yarn along the holes, tying a bow. There is room for at least one celebration for each month, but pages of the same size may be added as needed. (One plain page between each of the printed pages would be ideal!) Students, of course, may add their own drawings and decorative touches throughout the book. Inspiration and ideas will flow as students are introduced to the authors and their stories!

SHARING THE BOOKS

I'M IN CHARGE OF CELEBRATIONS

Read the book from beginning to end in one sitting. Allow plenty of time to enjoy the illustrations as you turn each page. Ask students to respond to the unusual idea of creating new kinds of holidays and celebrating seemingly insignificant happenings. (Together, you might make a list of events or ideas that could be celebrated as a class, such as the day everyone got 100 on the spelling test or the time the class rescued a baby bird, fallen from his nest outside your window.) Then ask students to sit quietly and observe silently the lovely illustrations of the book as you turn the pages slowly. Ask them to try to get a feel for Byrd Baylor's beloved desert and appreciate Peter Parnall's exceptional talent in capturing the desert scenery and animals on paper. If time allows, the enrichment art activity page, "Say It With Pictures," would be an excellent follow-up experience.

A TIME TO KEEP

This is a book to share slowly and intimately when there is time to talk about each page and the memories and images it evokes. The younger the students, the smaller the "doses" in which it may be presented. Older or more able students may share it in one or two sessions. Use a monthly calendar, turning its pages as you turn the parallel pages of the book to help students get a feel for the passing of time through a year. See if they can anticipate what events come next before you turn a page! However, the main focus is just to enjoy the book's story and illustrations and share the special moments it brings to children's minds – secrets of their own private "times to keep."

WORDS TO KNOW

celebrate	cactus	yuccas
coyote	ravines	choosy
whirlwinds	rainbow	desert
jackrabbit	favorite	tortoise
holiday	charades	birthday
sugaring	Maypole	party
firecracker	picnic	

January	May	September
February	June	October
March	July	November
April	August	December

CURRICULUM INTEGRATION

WRITING – "A Borrowed Notebook"

Make a copy of the "Borrowed Notebook" work sheet for each student. Reread together the third page of *I'm In Charge Of Celebrations* and discuss the process the author uses to choose a worthy occasion to celebrate. Ask students to choose a special event of their very own and use this "borrowed" page from the author's notebook to record their ideas.

LANGUAGE – "Celebrate Us All!"

Provide stencils or allow students to devise their own fancy lettering style to create large acrostics of their first names. (Letters should be no less than two inches high.) Provide white paper, colored pens, crayons, and rulers for the project so that names may be presented as illustrated below. When acrostics are finished, the teacher should hold up each paper, choose a letter, and think of a complimentary word or phrase that begins with that letter to describe that student. She or he may then write that word on the board and give the page to the student so that he or she may enter the word next to the appropriate letter in his or her name. When the teacher has addressed all names, students may trade papers among friends and classmates and enter additional adjectives to fill in one another's acrostics. The teacher may need to remain at the board to assist in spelling. Display finished products along a chalk tray, wall, or bulletin board.

ART – "Beautiful Borders"

Call attention to the attractive and unusual borders that frame the pages of the Tasha Tudor book. Notice that they are all different — they often include leaves, fruits, flowers, vines, ribbons, animals, and objects that illustrate the holiday theme. Supply paper; art supplies; a variety of tiny silk, paper, or plastic flowers; ribbon; laces; stickers; and confetti. Add students' old magazines, workbooks, and greeting cards that may be cut up for pictures. Ask students to choose a favorite month or event and create a border that might be used to frame a picture or memory of that time. Borders may be displayed or made into a class book, or students may fill in their frames at leisure and use them as covers for their own celebration books.

SOCIAL STUDIES/SCIENCE – "A Dozen Reasons To Celebrate"

Reproduce for each student a copy of the work sheet, "A Dozen Reasons To Celebrate." Explain that each of the twelve experiences described in the text takes place in one of five environments: the seaside, the desert, the mountains, the jungle, or at home. Students should cut the picture symbols from the bottom of the page and paste the appropriate symbol in the space provided at the beginning of each descriptive sentence.

MATH/SOCIAL STUDIES – "Birthdays Are Forever!"

Reproduce for each student a copy of the "Birthdays are Forever!" work sheet. Read it together as a class and discuss the concept of birthdays being "forever." Do at least one example of the problems together; then allow students to work the remaining problems independently. (**Note:** For more able students, original dates may be covered on the master, so students must research the name to find the birthdates.)

MATH/SPELLING – "Celebrate By Centimeters (Or Inches)!"

Reproduce a copy of the work sheet bearing this title for each student. Determine with students whether they will be working with inches or centimeters and provide rulers, pencils, and scissors. Be sure that all students understand and follow instructions. Do the activity yourself in advance so that you will know the final answer. (Students will whisper answers to you, and you will need to know how to respond!)

LANGUAGE/SPELLING – "Happy Word Celebration"

Give each student a copy of the work sheet with the crossword puzzle. Explain that the clues are provided in the tiny picture symbols. Words are printed out of order at the bottom of the page for assistance in spell checking! Puzzle words include the names of months and words from the "Words to Know" list at the beginning of the unit.

SOCIAL STUDIES/MATH – "A Part Of Me"

Ask each student to create or bring from home an object that reminds him or her of a special event or time to remember in his or her own life (other than a birthday, if possible). Plan brief "show and tell" sessions where students can share their objects and stories. Organize sharing sequentially, by months if you can, and write each student's name and event on the exact or appropriate date on the calendar.

ART ENRICHMENT – "Say It With Pictures"

Make a copy of the "Say It With Pictures" work sheet for each student. If you have not already done so during the initial presentation of the book, ask students to observe the illustrations silently as you page slowly through the book. When they have absorbed the "feel" of Peter Parnall's expert portrayal of Byrd Baylor's beloved desert, distribute the work sheet, and ask students to read and follow directions. **Note:** For younger students, you may want to place this list of events on the board: Dust Devil Day, Rainbow Celebration Day, Green Cloud Day, Coyote Day, Time of Falling Stars, New Year's Day.

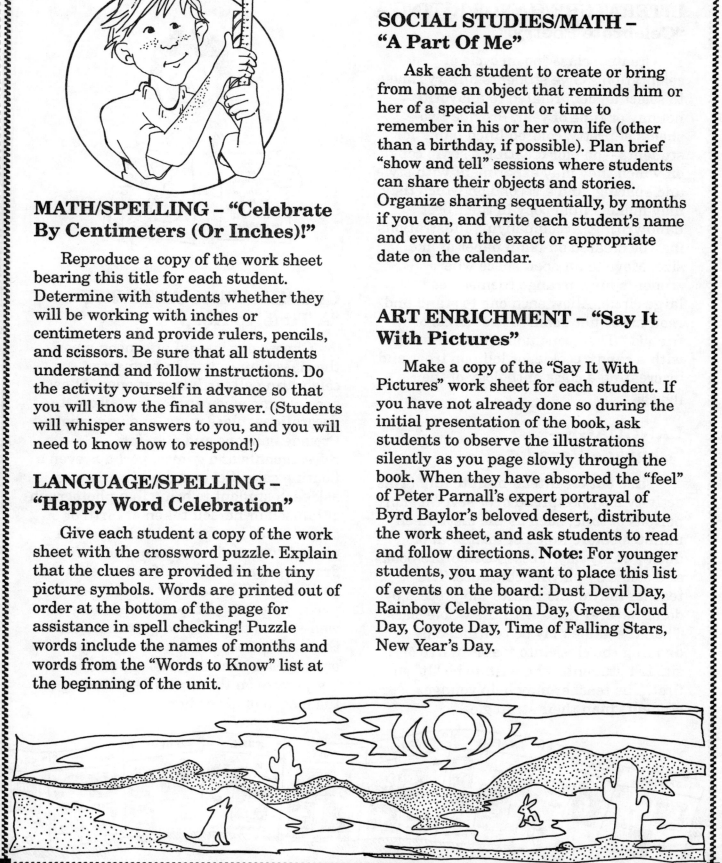

LITERATURE/HANDWRITING – "Celebrate Poetry!"

Create a class "poem cycle of celebration." Give students library time to select a poem related to a favorite holiday or time of year. Provide two sheets of pretty, colored lined paper for students — one for creating a scrap copy on which they may experiment with style and spacing, and a second on which they may make a final copy in their best handwriting. Accompanying illustrations may be created on plain paper of like size. Move to an open space where students may arrange themselves in a large circle. Allow each one to stand and read his or her poem to the "circle of friends." Then conclude the celebration with a candy, cookie, or lollipop treat and by creating a class anthology of the pages!

LANGUAGE – "Charade Parade"

Time out for fifteen-minute fun! (This activity may be spread over several short periods of time, such as the last fifteen minutes before lunch or dismissal or during rainy-day recess.) Celebrate books and songs by playing charades. The teacher may demonstrate the process by doing several titles with the whole class. Then the game may be continued by dividing the class into teams of five or six. Let students who wish to be "It" go first. The teacher may help younger students plan their strategies.

CULMINATING ACTIVITY – "A Time To Keep"

Choose one special afternoon when the class throws itself a big party, celebrating all birthdays at once. Allow a special time when students may create decorations, place mats, and party hats. Provide balloons and plan for refreshments and games, perhaps even a floating cake! Several days in advance, ask each student to bring in a photograph of himself or herself taken at birth or on one of his or her former birthdays. If a photo is not available, he or she may draw a picture of himself or herself at an earlier age. (The teacher must participate, too!) Prepare in advance a well-spaced time line to stretch across the wall or floor. As the main party activity, ask each student to place his or her picture on the time line according to the month of his or her birth.

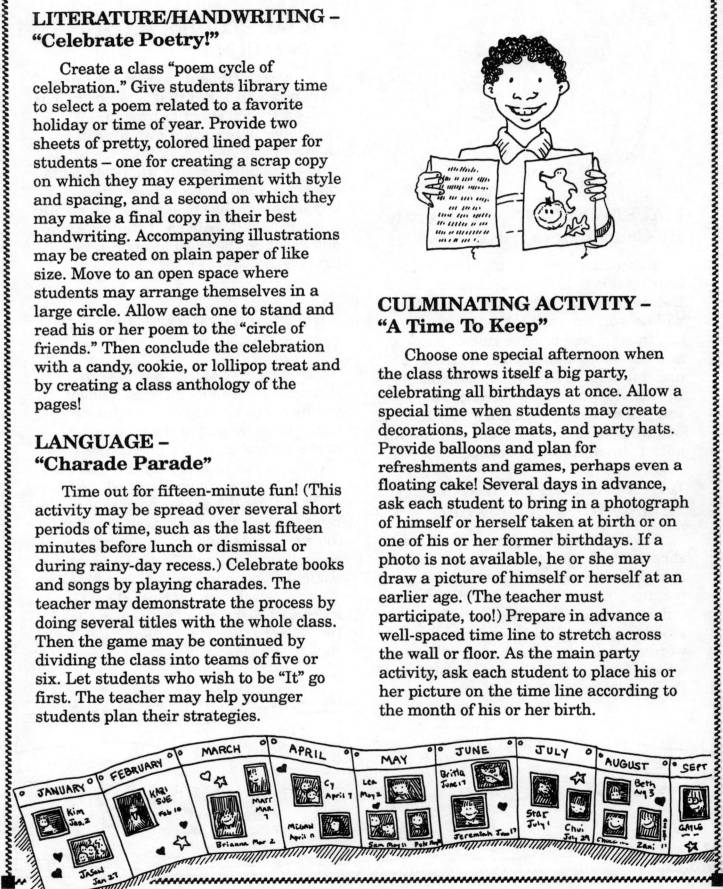

BORROWED NOTEBOOK

Name _____ Date _____

On the third page of her book, Byrd Baylor tells how she decides
if a day is a special one to celebrate. She explains how she keeps
track of celebration days in her notebook. Think about a special
occasion in the last few days or weeks of your life. What would
you like to celebrate? Use this pretend page from Byrd Baylor's
notebook. Enter the date and write about your celebration. (You
may write it as you think the author would write it, or you may
use a style all your own!)

A DOZEN REASONS TO CELEBRATE

Name _____ Date _____

Use your scissors to cut out the symbols on the solid lines at the bottom of "A Dozen Reasons To Celebrate," page 2. Read each sentence carefully. Decide whether the speaker is at the seaside, the desert, the mountains, the jungle, or at home. Paste the proper picture symbol beside each sentence. If you are unsure of your choice, the underlined key word(s) may give you a clue!

_____ A fiddler <u>crab</u> is scrambling over my toes!

_____ I discover a <u>sidewinder's</u> tracks in the <u>dust</u>!

_____ As I climb the <u>steep</u> path, I listen to the wind play harp-like tunes on the <u>tall</u> <u>pines</u>.

_____ I hear "someone" laughing at me. It's a <u>baboon</u>, mocking me from the top of a tall <u>banana</u> <u>tree</u>!

_____ I can find <u>no</u> <u>shade</u> from the burning sun except by standing with my arms straight up in the shadow of a <u>giant</u> <u>saguaro</u>.

_____ I find a family of <u>starfish</u> hiding between the rocks of the <u>seawall</u>.

A DOZEN REASONS TO CELEBRATE

My feet, hot and sore from <u>hiking</u>, share a cool, clear
bubbly stream with tiny silver fish, crawdads, and a
_____ long, green lizard.

I listen to the soft, funny, <u>comforting</u>
sounds of breathing, snoring, purring, and I am
_____ <u>content</u>, knowing we are all together and safe.

I spy the bright colorful blooms of <u>anemones</u>
_____ opening and closing with the movement of the <u>tide</u>.

I see a <u>camel</u> crossing the <u>flat</u> <u>horizon</u>.
_____ It is black against a bright orange sunset.

I am trying to nap in my <u>hammock</u>, but two noisy,
_____ sassy parrots keep me awake. It is <u>hot</u> <u>and</u> <u>sticky</u>!

I see playful <u>dolphins</u> leaping and diving, jumping and
_____ splashing. They think they are at a pool party!

seaside	mountain	jungle	desert	home	jungle
mountain	desert	seaside	desert	seaside	seaside

BIRTHDAYS ARE FOREVER!

Name _____ Date _____

You can keep having birthdays, even after you die!
People can continue celebrating the birthdays of those they love
and admire for hundreds of years. Aren't we funny? We even
celebrate the birthdays of people we have never met. Use your
math skills to see if you can tell how many candles should be on
the cake of these personalities THIS year!

GEORGE WASHINGTON
1732

MARTIN LUTHER KING
1929

THE CAT IN THE HAT
1957

YOUR FAVORITE AUTHOR

MOZART
1756

QUEEN ELIZABETH II
1926

ABRAHAM LINCOLN
1809

DR. SEUSS
1904

YOUR FAVORITE ILLUSTRATOR

WINNIE THE POOH
1926

CHARLIE BROWN
1950

YOUR TEACHER

CELEBRATE BY CENTIMETERS
(OR INCHES)!

Name _____ Date _____

You will need a ruler, a pencil, and scissors to do this work sheet. **Read the entire page before you begin.** Then go back to number 1 and follow each direction carefully.

1. Cut on the solid line to separate the candy stick from the rest of the page.

2. If April is the fourth month of the year, cut exactly **ONE inch or centimeter** off your candy stick.

3. If the second month has eight letters in its name, cut off exactly **TWO inches or centimeters**.

4. Cut off **ONE inch or centimeter** for every month whose name ends with the letters "**ber.**"

5. Cut off **1/2 inch or centimeter** for every month whose name begins with a vowel.

6. If four months have a name that begins with the letter **J**, cut off **TWO inches or centimeters.**

7. If four months have a name that ends with the letter **Y**, cut off **1/2 inch or centimeter.**

8. Measure the candy you have left. Whisper the number of inches or centimeters to your teacher. She or he will tell you if you are ready to celebrate your math and spelling skills.

HAPPY WORD CELEBRATION

Name _____ Date _____

Look at each picture symbol in the puzzle.
Choose the matching word from the list below and write it
carefully in the spaces following the symbol. Write ONE letter in
each space.

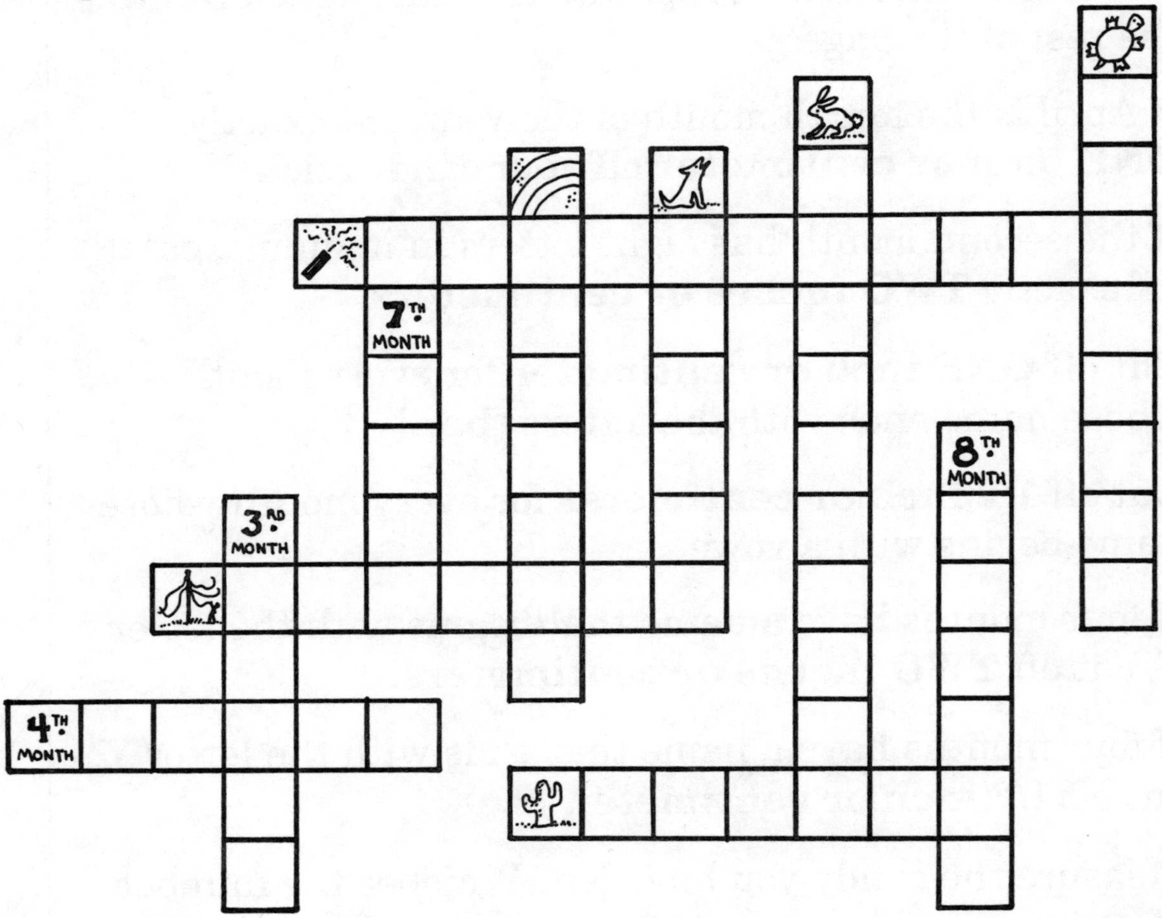

ACROSS:
Maypole
April
firecracker
cactus

DOWN:
March
August
July
jackrabbit

coyote
rainbow
tortoise

SAY IT WITH PICTURES

Name _____ Date _____

Peter Parnall, the illustrator of *I'm In Charge Of Celebrations*, read Byrd Baylor's word pictures and then created some lovely illustrations to go with those words. He is good at desert pictures! Page through the book. Don't read any words, but let your eyes feast on the pictures to get a feel for the desert. Then choose your favorite celebration from the story and use pens and pencils to create your own desert scene below. (You may give your drawing a title if you wish. Don't forget to sign it!)

February

JANUARY

APRIL

MARCH

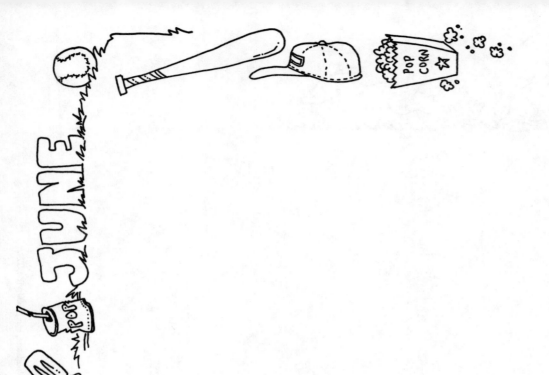

JUNE

MAY

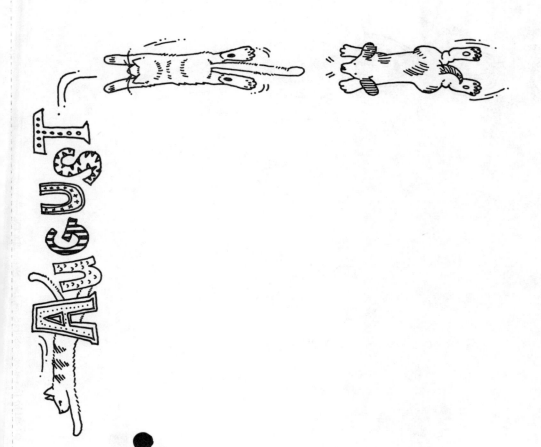

AUGUST

JULY

OCTOBER

SEPTEMBER

☆December☆

NOVEMBER

BIBLIOGRAPHY

A CHILD'S GARDEN OF VERSES by Robert Louis Stevenson. Illustrated by Tasha Tudor.
Rand McNally, 1981.

CLOUDY WITH A CHANCE OF MEATBALLS by Judi Barrett. Illustrated by
Ron Barrett. *Atheneum*, 1978.

FAINT FROGS FEELING FEVERISH written and illustrated by Lilian Obligado.
Viking Press, 1983.

FREDERICK written and illustrated by Leo Lionni. *Pantheon Books*, 1967.

HECKEDY PEG by Audrey Wood. Illustrated by Don Wood.
Harcourt Brace and Jovanovich, 1987.

HOW THE GRINCH STOLE CHRISTMAS written and illustrated by Dr. Seuss.
Random House, 1957.

HOW MANY DAYS TO AMERICA? by Eve Bunting. Illustrated by Beth Peck.
Clarion Books, 1988.

I'M IN CHARGE OF CELEBRATIONS by Byrd Baylor. Illustrated by Peter Parnall.
Charles Scribner's Sons, 1986.

JIMMY'S BOA BOUNCES BACK by Trinka Hakes Noble. Illustrated by Steven Kellogg.
Dial Books, 1984.

THE LEPRECHAUN'S STORY by Richard Kennedy. Illustrated by Marcia Sewall.
E.P. Dutton, 1979.

MISS NELSON IS MISSING by Harry Allard. Illustrated by James Marshall.
Houghton Mifflin Company, 1977.

MISS RUMPHIUS written and illustrated by Barbara Cooney. *Viking Penguin, Inc.*, 1982.

OH! THE THINKS YOU CAN THINK! written and illustrated by Dr. Seuss.
Random House, 1975.

THE RELATIVES CAME by Cynthia Rylant. Illustrated by Stephen Gammell.
Bradbury Press, 1985.

A TIME TO KEEP by Tasha Tudor. *Rand McNally*, 1977.

WIFRID GORDON MCDONALD PARTRIDGE by Mem Fox. Illustrated by Julie Vivas.
American edition by *Kane/Midler*, 1985.

OTHER SOURCES

CHICKENS AREN'T THE ONLY ONES written and illustrated by Ruth Heller.
Grosset and Dunlap, 1981.

SING A SONG OF POPCORN by Beatrice Schenk. Illustrated by Marcia Brown. *Scholastic,*
1988.

THE SNOWY DAY written and illustrated by Ezra Jack Keats. *Viking*, 1963.